True Light

Ordinary People on the Extraordinary Spiritual Path of Sukyo Mahikari

Leena Banerjee Brown, PhD

with contributions from Roger L. Beck, PhD

Light
on
Light
press

Cover photo by Deb Mukharji taken on Canon A1 with f2 135 mm lens on Kodachrome 64 film: While trekking in the Himalaya, Deb Mukharji sensed the light turning mellow as the clouds began to lift one gray September afternoon. He rushed up the trail hoping to get a glimpse of the mountain and was rewarded by the glowing tip of Nanda Devi just moments before the shadows crept up. Named after the consort of Shiva, Nanda Devi not only dominates the skyline, but also the folklore and mythology of the Garhwal region, which is itself a rich storehouse of mythological associations linked to the ancient Sanskrit epic Mahabharata.

Books may be purchased through booksellers or by contacting Sacred Stories Publishing.

True Light: Ordinary People on the Extraordinary Spiritual Path of Sukyo Mahikari
Leena Banerjee Brown, PhD
with contributions from Roger L. Beck, PhD

Tradepaper ISBN: 978-1-945026-74-4
Electronic ISBN: 978-1-945026-75-1
Library of Congress Control Number: 2021930981

Published by Light on Light Press
An imprint of Sacred Stories Publishing, Fort Lauderdale, FL

Printed in the United States of America

To the memory of my father,
the late Lieutenant General Ashish Banerjee, PVSM
*whose name **ashish** means blessing, as he was.*

Table of Contents

THE DALAI LAMA

Foreword

A spiritual journey is essentially devoted to developing our genuine concern for others. We cultivate positive qualities such as patience, compassion and loving kindness, while countering negative mental qualities like anger and attachment, which cause us unhappiness and inflict suffering on those around us.

The benefit we derive from practicing more altruism will be an increase in our mental as well as our physical wellbeing. The process can be thought of as "mental hygiene"; just as we must attend to our physical hygiene, it is important that we improve both our heart and mind to develop inner peace.

Dr. Leena Banerjee Brown's book is an account of the spiritual journeys of a few practitioners who describe how their own happiness and wellbeing have increased as a result of their effort to help others. I hope that this book will be an inspiration to the many who make their way along their spiritual paths.

1 February 2021

Preface

Long before Roger Beck and I met one another, each of us was separately introduced to the same spiritual practice and spiritual path. For him in 1986 and for me in 2002, initially, our new spiritual practice functioned like a small add-on to our lives. But as the practices began to transform us, the path became central to both of our daily lives. That's what this book is about: what happens when ordinary people embark on an extraordinary path by integrating spiritual practice into daily life. Roger's path and mine happen to converge on the practices of Sukyo Mahikari—an organization devoted to the divine inspiration revealed to 20th-century Japanese teacher Kōtama Okada—yet we strongly identify with millions of people pursuing countless other paths for whom the transformative experience of spiritual practice is equally powerful. I speak for all of the people whose stories are held in the pages of this book when I say we're not interested in promoting one path over another. We simply must share our stories lest we greedily hoard the blessings we've received through spiritual practice.

If you want to read a detailed description of the history, mission, and vision of Sukyo Mahikari, we recommend an excellent book written by Dr. Sidney Chang called *God's Light and Universal Principles for All Humanity: An Introduction to Sukyo Mahikari*. If you'd like to walk beside people who have experienced inner and outer transformation through the practice of giving and receiving True Light (which we sometimes just call "Light") and bear witness to their stories in the context of your own life, the book you now hold in your hand will be a fine companion for you. Less a treatise on Sukyo Mahikari and more a narrative compilation of many personal experiences and insights, it speaks to the impact of deep spiritual practice on individual lives and minds, the natural environment, and the world as a whole. Although our stories reflect a particular spiritual practice, our experiences suggest that integration of spirituality in daily life holds tremendous potential to change lives for the better, whatever the chosen spiritual practice may be. And so, we offer here a general endorsement of integrating spirituality in daily life by way of sharing a range of stories emerging from a specific path.

It's not uncommon for people to begin a spiritual journey as a consequence of some sort of physical, mental, or emotional loss (or the perception thereof). Coincidentally, for both Roger and me, the first leg of our spiritual journey coincided with a trip to our respective doctor's offices whereby physical health challenges served as a window into the spiritual dimension of life. As we each recovered from chronic ailments, not through medical treatment alone but primarily through spiritual practice, our lives were transformed. We weren't opposed to choosing medical options; that's where the journey began. Roger and I both remained open to using traditional medicine when needed, but it was the powerful impact of spiritual practice that awakened us. The blessings we received left us with a deep and pure sense of gratitude and a desire to pay it forward to others, hoping they would reap great benefits as well.

But improved health was only the beginning. Over time, as spiritual practice became integrated into our daily lives, we began to recognize a deeper transformation. Just as the practices we regularly engaged in removed physical impurities that had caused us bodily harm, these practices began to gradually eliminate physical, mental, and spiritual impurities. And just as the removal of physical impurities restored our physical health, through the removal of mental and spiritual impurities we became more conscious of our true selves—spiritual beings connected with the perfect will of God. We eventually understood that through our spiritual practice we were being filled with wisdom, love, forgiveness, altruism, and a refined sense of our personal will flowing to us from something much larger than our individual selves.

Step by step, we studied universal principles like gratitude, acceptance, and humility, and worked to incorporate these principles in our thoughts and actions. Our innermost attitudes began to change, which supported changes in the boundaries of our consciousness. Gradually, our lives were more and more directed toward God and centered on altruism. We have seen impacts on many aspects of our lives such as well-being, education, and connection with nature through the natural environment, agriculture, and food.

It would not be an exaggeration to say our lives have been significantly transformed for the better, allowing us to live with a deep and authentic sense of purpose. The changes we've experienced continually fill us with surprise, wonder, and gratitude. And, of course, we are not alone in this experience. So, I have invited a number of people from the greater Sukyo Mahikari community to join us by sharing their experiences. Each of us has his or her own unique experiences, consistent with the truth that each individual's needs for spiritual growth are unique. At the same time we deeply share common ground. We have learned to rely on divine action, however one wishes to define or describe it, to make the best arrangements for each person's growth, including the pace at which growth occurs.

Awareness of this deeply personal relationship with the divine comes with a caveat: there is simply no way to name the source of this divine action that would adequately recognize the nameless quality of the source of all. Please forgive any disrespect or clumsiness on my part as I choose to apply the proper noun "God" to describe That Which Cannot Be Described. Language is sorely limited in its ability to convey the ineffable, but after consulting with several friends and editors, I have decided that the simplest way to go is "God." If this nomenclature causes you any discomfort or disagreement, please feel free to mentally substitute a word that is preferable to you. Some have suggested

"Universal Will", "Ground of Being", "Source", "Comforter", or "Divine Parent." I'm told the founders of 12-Step recovery programs wrestled with the same desire to offer inclusive terminology to describe the entity they knew as "God." In the interest of reaching as many people as possible with their message of freedom from addiction, they settled upon the phrase "Higher Power." Please know that I share their desire to be as inclusive and general as possible, but I have returned to the word "God" in the name of simplicity and non-distraction.

Reading about others' spiritual transformation can be a strange experience. As you thumb through the pages of this book, you may ask yourself "Why should I trust what this author has to say about such deeply personal, sensitive things?" Or you may wonder "How will I ever live up to the amazing stories these people share?" Or you may find it difficult to believe the miraculous transformations documented and conveyed through the written word. I can certainly relate to these sentiments. And so, I simply invite you to read these stories through the lens of your own experience. Spirituality is indeed a deeply personal topic. Your spirit, your mind, and your body are just as important to this book as are the spirits, minds, and bodies of the people who have contributed to its content. Please consider yourself an integral part of this compilation, in which your personal stories are welcome alongside those you are reading. Some parts of the book may resonate deeply with you, while others may leave you scratching your head. Isn't that how life is?! The spiritual life is equally complex and diverse, yet many universal truths unite us.

As you read these stories, may you be blessed as you consider the role of spiritual practice in your own life. This is my humble wish for you, dear reader.

Dr. Leena Banerjee Brown, 2021

Introductory Words

Wayne Teasdale, in *The Mystic Heart: Discovering a Universal Spirituality in the World's Religions*, wrote that in the near future diverse leaders, from many cultures, would come forward proposing holistic and universal understandings of the world's great wisdom traditions. As the global interspiritual discussion has evolved, many have recognized that among such major figures in the global evolution of a universal spirituality, a notable one is Japan's Kōtama Okada. Kōtama Okada is the founder of the global Sukyo Mahikari movement which, as "Sukyo Mahikari Centers for Spiritual Development," originated in Japan and has since spread expansively worldwide, today having over one million members and centers in seventy-five nations.

Like other pioneering figures of our modern day who became pathfinders in their own unique ways, Kōtama Okada's roots stem from a particular national and cultural religious heritage, but also from a unique personal direct experience which led him to not only articulate his universal teachings but create a global community around them. Anyone who familiarizes themself with the foundational writings of Kōtama Okada immediately recognizes their similarity with the language, worldview, cosmology, and yes—even the general view of the future—now commonly associated with the phenomena of interfaith and interspirituality around the world. These include, in short, a whole-world global perspective on the shared heritage of all spiritual traditions and perennial philosophies, the desire that they help create "a world that works for all" in a cosmopolitan global age, and, in that, emphasize shared universal principles and advise universal action steps that are deeply holistic and all-inclusive—much akin to the ancient and often nature-based wisdoms of indigenous peoples.

History of Kōtama Okada and Sukyo Mahikari

Kōtama Okada's birth was accompanied by a mystical occurrence. His mother had a dream in which she said she experienced a message from a "Messenger Deity" (or spirit) from the ancestral lineage to which she belonged. In fact, Kōtama Okada was descended (on both his mother's and father's sides) from two of the three lineages of "great unifiers" recorded in Japanese history— Nobunaga Oda and Ieyasu Tokugawa. These two lineages of military and political leaders of the Warring Period (1467-1568 CE) and Post-Warring Period of Japan were instrumental in unifying the nation. This unification led to a period of internal peace, political stability, and economic growth that lasted three-hundred years. Okada is thus seen, historically, as shouldering the responsibilities of his heritage—the reputation, stature, and influence of his ancestral lineage.

This background is reflected in Okada's brilliant military career, which was cut short by the sudden onset of severe illness. Gravely ill, he was told by medical specialists that he had only three years to live and he was transferred to the reserves. Forced to reshape his life, Okada liquidated his entire ancestral inheritance and invested these resources in a number of business ventures. In a relatively short time the companies he created became so successful that he was nationally recognized as an important business leader. In addition, contrary to expectations, his physical condition improved considerably and, eventually, all signs of his serious illness disappeared.

In August 1945, however, all of his companies were destroyed in the air raids concluding World War II. Okada found himself physically exhausted with a mountain of debt. Also homeless, he spent his nights sleeping under a bridge.

As he reflected on all of this, he came to deep personal conclusions about what had befallen him. First, he felt he had forgotten God in the midst of his previous successes. He also felt there was need for him to compensate for negative karma associated with the warring activities of his ancestors in how they had carried out their efforts and activities to unite Japan. This was the beginning of Kōtama Okada's personal spiritual evolution.

Typifying how the history of our world's religions has often unfolded, and also Wayne Teasdale's emphasis on the importance of "prophetic voice" in his now well-known Nine Elements of a Universal Spirituality[1], Okada was then guided by what he interpreted as revelatory experiences. The most important of these occurred on February 22nd, 1959 when he fell into a deep unconscious state for five days. For Okada, the content in this experience was numinous, meaning it was experienced as both a direct personal epiphany and a directive to personal action. The experiences of February 1959 led Okada to conclude that a calling, a mission, had been revealed to him—to establish a spiritual movement that would promulgate into the world a new wave of universal teachings.

Further typifying the origins of many of our world's influential spiritual movements, Okada at first questioned his own experiences and tested them, both personally and with his surrounding community. He began his new work by combining the message of his emerging teachings with his business skills, establishing cottage industries to serve the impoverished people around him. The success of these businesses, and their unquestionable linkage to the optimism and hope found in his teachings, increased certainty about his sense of calling and established him as a trusted community and spiritual leader. This gave further confidence to Okada and his followers about the efficacy and importance of their novel and innovative beliefs. These included a view of the Creator's universal laws and a future plan framed in an emphasis on universal principles and advised universal action steps, a way of living more in harmony with nature and natural laws, and spiritual practices that provided deep senses not only of personal well-being but of collective harmony. In the face of a perilous time and threatening future, these promised the chance, Okada taught, for humanity to make a "Great U-turn" back to basics.

Typifying again the history of many new religious movements, Okada continued to have directly personal experiences concerning his sense of calling, which further shaped his work. Some experiences were dramatic or even severe, including one concerning what became his new first name: "Kōtama." In this direct experience he was told:

> You will be made to speak the depth of the teachings, which was not revealed before. The Spirit of Truth has entered you. You shall speak what you hear. The time of heaven has come. Rise. Your name shall be Kōtama. Raise your hand. The world shall enter severe times.[2]

Okada was surprised by this, and other experiences that followed, but he elected to continue following his calling. This devotion soon led him to discover friendships among the adherents and leadership of ancient Shinto (the ancient indigenous spiritual tradition of Japan) which, again to his surprise, revealed a deep context within historical Shinto prophecy by which he could further understand the meaning of his experiences. Some priests from a tradition of esoteric Shinto suggested that he participate in a series of well-established ritual tests to determine the authenticity of his experiences. He agreed.[3] The Shinto priests were interested because there exists in Shinto a teaching that a person with the mission of *Yo* would appear on earth at about this time.

The Shinto tests were repeated several times, beginning in June 1960, and each time they produced the same result, not only convincing the priests but also confirming through their own inquiries the validity of many of Okada's predictions. Thus, Okada, now known as Kōtama Okada, became the founder of a new religious movement that was not only prophetic in its cosmology—looking toward the world's globalized future—but also innovative in fresh methods of personal and collective spiritual practice. These practices, which became known as the art of True Light, were both uniquely nuanced and akin to the energy related practices of a number of the world religions. Typifying the origin histories of many spiritual traditions, the art of True Light – the purification of spirit, mind, and body with divine energy, through Okada's movement, achieved such positive results in the lives of adherents that the movement and its teachings spread quickly and widely.

Kōtama Okada's Message

According to Okada's teachings, it is important now for society to nurture spirit-centered people who can take on the responsibility of being pioneers in the twenty-first century. Seeing the global landscape emerging after the World Wars, Okada wanted to share a vision that transcended human-made barriers and boundaries between ethnic groups, cultures, religions, and nationalities. He clearly perceived that such teachings could help humankind awaken to a global sense of oneness and the desire to pursue a planet-wide civilization based on unity consciousness.

According to these teachings, the Creator has a plan that spans billions of years. The ultimate goal of the plan is that human beings, who are the Creator's children, will create a heavenly civilization on earth, a civilization that is a physical reflection of the highest of ideals, those that have historically been associated with the divine, where people live in accordance with perennial teachings of love and thus enjoy eternal prosperity. In this cosmology, after providing the earth with its bountiful supply of natural resources, the Creator intended its human inhabitants to use their diverse talents and physical skills to properly utilize and steward the earth's resources. This is a co-creator cosmology in which humans have an important and highly responsible role to fulfill.

Because of this context, Okada's cosmology can be described as a developmental cosmology, much in tune with the modern views of the evolutionary consciousness, integral, and developmental movements. It takes into account that, historically, humanity would ebb and flow through different paradigms of attainment, one replacing another. There would be appropriate times for materialistic development followed by appropriate times for the reintegration of spiritual and moral values. Thus, as history has shown, people developed civilizations in many parts of the world in which the quest to produce and accumulate material things played an important role. In the process of developing these civilizations, people often became excessively materialistic and frequently exploited other people and nature. Okada said, for instance, that by placing material values above ethical, moral, or spiritual values, people would end up polluting not only the earth, the oceans, and the atmosphere, but also their core values—their souls. If people continue to live contrary to universal principles, he said, it would become increasingly difficult for them to establish a sustainable civilization on earth. Indeed, he said, if humanity continues to ultimately travel along the purely materialistic path, one day this path might lead to the destruction of humankind.

But in turn, he said, if humanity would take responsibility for the repercussions of its materialistic achievements and return to a deep sense of ethics, morals, and spiritual values, there could be a healthy movement on to the next stage of history. This stage of history, he said, could be one of a sustainable and healthy global civilization, one dedicated to the well-being of all. According to Okada's teachings, in 1962 humankind entered a new era, a period of major transition, a time wherein spiritual wisdom and values would begin to take precedence over material values and eventually encompass them. When he founded the Mahikari organization in 1959, Kōtama Okada's intention was to find and nurture people who could become seed persons, or pioneers, for the new spiritual civilization. He hoped that such pioneers would elevate themselves spiritually by truly dedicating themselves to practicing divine principles in daily life. Through their efforts to work for the accomplishment of such a future for the world, seed people, he said, could help create the best possible outcome for an ethical, moral, and heart-centered global civilization at this critical stage in history. This vision is one that has helped make the modern vision of the Sukyo Mahikari movement inspiring to millions.

Day-to-Day Life

Typifying a spiritual community for the global age, Sukyo Mahikari is an organization where people from all walks of life and different backgrounds come together to develop themselves spiritually so they can realize their true potential as human beings. By developing themselves spiritually, people have the opportunity to improve their lives and to enjoy better health and well-being. In addition, they have the opportunity to find an effective way to help others and to live in greater harmony with their family, colleagues, and their environment. Helping others and living in harmony with one's surroundings are some of the best ways to achieve personal growth and real happiness. A major principle of the movement is its commitment to green living and sustainability. For instance, its New York City center is a model LEED-certified green building celebrated by designers and architects worldwide for its pioneering approaches to buildings and building materials.

In the day-to-day life of its adherents, the lifestyle tools that Sukyo Mahikari would like to share with everyone include its spiritual energy practices—the art of True Light—and its teachings concerning universal principles that could achieve the type of future world that so many long for. For Sukyo Mahikari adepts, the practice of giving and receiving divine Light allows people to gradually awaken to the existence of the spiritual dimension—the world of the subtle and spiritual realms and the reality of God, Source, or Creator, the subtle vibrations of their soul or true self, as well as the subtle vibrations of their innermost attitude and those of others. The integration of these felt experiences and understandings has a profound influence on human life. It leads to appreciation of the close interconnection and relationship between spirit, mind, and body, and particularly the importance of one's inner life. Regarding day-to-day life, a major Sukyo Mahihari principle is expressed as the principle of "spirit first, mind next, body follows." Utilizing both the teachings and practices, people can cultivate a positive and holistic attitude and elevate the vibration of their innermost attitude in the direction of pure, altruistic love and harmony. As a result, they can be people of high self-esteem and confidence and find deeper purpose and meaning in their lives.

The Interspirituality of Okada's Teachings

Of particular interest in this time of prominent interspiritual, integral, and holistic movements is the major premise of the message from Okada's teachings concerning all religions rediscovering their common origin. Another is Okada's insistence on emphasizing, in a direct manner, teachings concerning the profound interconnectedness of everything, not only in what we know from modern science, but in emphasizing the direct experience of the contemplative or mystical dimension of human consciousness.[4] For Okada, and the Sukyo Mahikari tradition, this means truly holistic and integral approaches to all aspects of life and living. It is these aspects of Okada's teachings that are so fully in tune with the entire landscape of modern holistic movements such as Integral, Spiral Dynamics, Whole-World View, Prosocial, Good of the Whole, and so many more seen around the world today. Readers of Okada's works and commentaries on them from across his movement are often surprised by the similarity of his language and worldview with modern interspiritual and integral writers like Wayne Teasdale and Ken Wilber.

Okada's direct manner of how to view spiritual experience defined his stated mission—to give people, through their connection with their experience of God, the opportunity to utilize the practice of True Light.[5] Because of the consistency between ancient Shinto teachings and those that had arisen independently through Okada's personal experiences, Sukyo Mahikari gained respect within the historical understanding of Japan's rich religious heritage. The fact that the revelations confirmed by the ritual tests were identical to those received by him was a surprise to the Shinto priests. However, this became part of a new and general direction in the understanding of new religious movements in Japan among modern religious scholars. A larger landscape has emerged in which Sukyo Mahikari and a number of other modern religious movements in Japan—because of their implicit historical and cultural relationship to the larger history of religions in Japan—are today often generically identified by religious scholars as the New Shinto religious movements. In Okada's case, indeed, these independent tests of him and his teachings by the traditional Shinto communities later proved to be an important factor in persuading many influential people in Japan to accept Okada's vision and collaborate with him.

Sukyo Mahikari in Further Perspective

It is not a surprise to find yet another global movement whose principles and visions mirror the emerging sense of an arising Interspiritual Age as envisioned in the interspiritual work of Wayne Teasdale and many other modern interfaith and interspiritual writers and leaders. Modern interfaith and interspiritual communities recognize over fifty such pioneers over several centuries whose works emphasize the commonalities between them all.[6] Kōtama Okada's message mirrors that of all the major interspiritual pioneers. *Sukyo* itself means "the universal laws established by the Creator at the time of the Creation so that all things in the universe can prosper eternally," and *Mahikari* (being a combination of *Ma* which is Truth and *hikari* which is Light) means "True Light," the Light of the Creator which purifies all things.

Because the objective of Sukyo Mahikari is to help people awaken to universal (or divine) principles, and to encourage them to respect and practice these principles in daily life, it is an example of today's global trend toward expression of universal truth and the hope for a healthy global civilization. Typifying the vision of the entire pantheon of historical interspiritual pioneers, the movement built on the vision of Kōtama Okada is one of holistic interspiritual principles, joining in one universal cosmology the realms of science, religion, education, history, politics, and the many other things that people pursue in order to make the world potentially a happier and better place to live. Interestingly—but not surprisingly, given the vision of an Interspiritual Age—Sukyo Mahikari originally sprang from the roots of one culture, indeed the ancient wisdom traditions of Japanese culture. It is precisely because of this ancient rooting that it simultaneously represents something born anew—by the universal views of its founder. This has caused Sukyo Mahikari to succeed worldwide. We hope we can look toward Sukyo Mahikari, among many other movements like it worldwide today, to lead humanity toward the kind of sustainable, ethical, and moral world for which everyone in their heart of hearts yearns.

Dr. Kurt Johnson, 2021

Chapter 1

Giving and Receiving True Light

The spiritual path of Sukyo Mahikari is compatible with many religious paths. If one meets the practices of giving and receiving True Light as a Christian, one may remain Christian along the path. If one meets the practices of giving and receiving True Light as a Hindu, one may remain Hindu along the path. If one meets the practices of giving and receiving True Light as a Muslim, one may remain Muslim along the path. If one meets the practices of giving and receiving True Light as a Buddhist, one may remain Buddhist along the path. And so it goes for all spiritual paths and practices. If one meets the practices of giving and receiving True Light with no specific religious or spiritual path, one need not adopt a specific tradition to encounter God on the path of Sukyo Mahikari.

Following a spiritual path develops the mind's reflective capacity to shift our innermost attitudes from material-centeredness to spirit-centeredness. As a result, we more easily perceive the deeper meaning in our experiences and others' experiences. This helps us become more conscious of the connection between the true self, in the depths of our minds and bodies, and God. We are also better able to empathically connect with others' experiences and true selves, making others feel deeply seen and heard. Our relationships with others are enhanced, contributing to our well-being. Such development of our human core nurtures our sense of connection with nature (and its stewardship) and with humanity.

Not only do tangible benefits flow to those individuals who integrate spirituality in daily life, but also—as more and more people do this—huge benefits will accrue to humanity as a whole, to science, and to nature. The shift from material-centeredness to spirit-centeredness broadens the human heart and mind, bringing to consciousness the genuine, deep, and meaningful connections between humans, as well as deep harmony between humans and nature. People who discover their true selves will develop the motivation to fulfill their true purpose. These inner changes manifest externally in countless ways, including restoration of the environment, adoption of less toxic agricultural practices, and production of less contaminated, healthier food.

Becoming conscious of our own connection to God makes us conscious of others' connections to God as well. Because all human beings are born into divine connection, we recognize that we are all spiritual siblings. Our increased feeling of love toward others makes it easier to foster true harmony and peace in our daily lives. War, conflict, and forceful taking from others become less tolerable for us. We recognize the significance and value of each person's contribution to the well-being of the whole. By integrating spirituality in daily life, we participate in the improvement of the overall condition of humanity.

Everybody's Spiritual Journey Starts Somewhere

It's fascinating to hear peoples' stories of how they took their first steps on a path of daily spiritual practice. Some people describe a deep shift in perspective caused by a global event, like the tragic day known as 9-11, or a natural disaster like the 2011 tsunami, or even a deeply personal loss of a loved one. Others are moved by a poignant experience with nature, a sunset that spoke directly to their soul, or a pilgrimage to a significant spiritual shrine. Others may not be able to pinpoint the exact moment they decided to devote themselves to daily spiritual practice, but instead, over time came to recognize they had joined millions of other spiritual practitioners by simply walking in their footsteps toward a life well-lived.

I share my story with you not to impress you with its significance, but to befriend you through its authenticity. With his permission, I'd also like to share with you parts of my friend Roger Beck's story as he has shared it with me. While he and I hold much in common as people whose lives have been transformed by our dedication to spiritual practice, our stories begin in very different places. And to add to the diversity of the larger story of Sukyo Mahikari, I'd also like to share snippets of stories from a handful of friends and family who, when they heard I had begun to write about my experience giving and receiving True Light, generously offered their own reflections.

Everyone's spiritual practice starts somewhere. It's humbling to know that we are all really beginners, in the sense that developing a spiritual practice is a process that reveals itself progressively. By this I mean the farther we go on the spiritual journey, the more we realize how far there is to go! But it is a joyous journey, one definitely worth considering. I think most of us can look back into our earliest childhood memories and remember spiritual moments or insights that came to us organically. For me, times spent with my grandparents hold many such memories.

In 2002, during a particularly busy time in my life, the intermittent seasonal allergies I had suffered since young adulthood took a turn for the worse. While I'm grateful my extreme hay fever was not a life threatening disease, it was a life altering chronic condition that was limiting my ability to engage in life as I wished to. During a particularly severe bout, my doctor prescribed a course of steroids. The medicine had the desired response of reducing inflammation and managing the symptoms of my allergies, but my body spoke to me in very clear terms as the corticosteroids entered my system. It was as if an internal fire alarm went off warning me of extreme toxicity. I didn't fully appreciate the significance of this moment, but I did recognize my body's response to this drug as a spontaneous moment of deep spiritual insight. It was as if I was seeing through the window of my soul. And so, I resolved that no matter how allergies might plague me in the future, and despite the pressure of being a professor of psychology, consulting psychologist, wife, and mother of three small children, I would not ingest such toxic medicine again. It was a pledge to myself made in a moment of deep clarity. Although I did not realize it then, it was also a pledge to honor and preserve the sacred gift of my true self, in both mind and body.

Looking back, I'm deeply grateful a relatively benign health crisis was enough to get my attention. Countless memoirs have been written by people who were awakened to the spirit-mind-body connection through extreme suffering or even near death experiences. What is extraordinary about my story is its beautiful ordinariness. I am not some chosen being who was singled out by fate to walk a rarified path. Quite the contrary. I'm an ordinary person who was blessed enough to be paying attention to the subtle yet clear message that forever changed my life.

But my allergies persisted. Without the steroids to keep my nasal passages, sinuses, and lungs clear, I sneezed and dripped my way through another season of hay fever. The beautiful flowers and trees of my Southern California home taunted me as I juggled clients, students, and family with one hand while reaching for a handkerchief with the other. So when a sympathetic colleague looked into my bloodshot eyes and asked me if I would be willing to participate in an experiment that might alleviate my symptoms, I was enthusiastically receptive. But this time it wasn't a drug. I was introduced to the spiritual practice of True Light taught by Sukyo Mahikari.

The first time I received True Light, I experienced profound connection with the infinite. It was an experience of coming alive to the depths of truth, love, and harmony within. It was powerful! I felt as though I had been laboring up the mountain of my daily life and then suddenly I was given a drink of water from a mountain spring—so pure, so thirst-quenching, and deeply refreshing. The energy and experience were so powerful it was like being fully immersed in water I was simultaneously drinking. On the physical plane, while I did not ask for water it was suddenly given. On the spiritual plane, it felt as if all my life's efforts and those of my forebears had been undertaken ultimately to reach that mountain spring.

I think so many of us are walking up mountains like this every day. When my colleague offered to help me with my allergies, I was grateful to explore something beyond what doctors had prescribed, something different from all the other holistic methods and remedies I had tried. But it was truly my colleague's love, care, and attentiveness as a person that opened my mind and heart to the transformation available to us all. Sukyo Mahikari is simply the messenger. It's the True Light that truly transforms.

I now know it was pure compassion that motivated my colleague Lorri to introduce me to True Light. Lorri was the kindest of people to work with—always thoughtful even when our work was challenging and stressful. I remember the day Lorri suggested I receive True Light. I was feeling small and tired under the burden of my ongoing allergies and an exceptionally difficult caseload. As a consulting psychologist at a Southern California non-profit where more and more high risk, substance addicted, developmentally challenged babies, children, and adults were being served, it was easy to become discouraged. That day I was catching up on paperwork at Lorrie's office, which was in a lovely old Spanish-style adobe mansion with a red clay tile roof and a stand of palm trees towering above. Lorri strode into the room dressed in a long, flowing coral-colored suit jacket and black silken slacks. Her eyes shone even brighter than the fine jewelry that accented her stylish wardrobe, filling the room with beauty, optimism, and hope. The energy of the room immediately shifted when Lorri arrived—like a ray of sunshine, as they say. When she saw my tired face and weary smile, she leaned over and, gently touching my shoulder, said "Why don't you receive some Light today?" Without hesitation I followed her into an adjoining room with warm wood-toned wainscoting adorning the lower walls and soft white upper walls and ceilings that drew my eyes toward the rustic tin chandelier that hung over a massive walnut conference table. Lorri introduced me to her friend Eiko, an older, shorter woman dressed in a plain skirt and top similar to what I was wearing. I immediately sensed Eiko's warmth, and soon thereafter recognized a loving presence about her that was quite immovable. I took a seat at the table with very little idea of what was about to happen.

I knew Lorri and Eiko had been good friends for many years and that they were both members of a spiritual community with a name that sounded Japanese to me. I trusted Lorri, and although I had just met Eiko, I settled in the chair in front of her and within a few minutes felt relaxed and comfortable in her presence. When Eiko invited me to receive Light, I was entirely ready to experience something new. I didn't know what it would be, but I was open. Facing her with my eyes closed, I listened as she chanted a powerful prayer of purification asking that I be purified with True Light. Then she radiated invisible energy, True Light, from the palm of her hand held about a foot in front of my forehead. She radiated True Light first to my forehead, then to the back of my head and neck, then to my lower back in the vicinity of my kidneys. The process lasted for about half an hour. At the end of the session, we each offered a prayer of gratitude to God, and thanked each other.

I felt dynamically activated inside, but was speechless at first—unable to articulate this experience which was truly beyond words. How could I communicate the pristine, powerful silence inside me? Slowly, by the end of the day, my energy level rose and my breathing became clear and unencumbered by the allergies that had been plaguing me. I cycled through the same experience several times over several months. When professional and family life challenges would cause my stress levels to rise, my immunities would fall and I would begin sneezing and my sinus passages would become totally blocked again. Then I would be lucky enough to receive True Light for about half an hour. Again, by the end of the day I would not only be free from hay fever and sinusitis, I would be energized and refreshed. I would feel happy and healthy.

Although my husband David was skeptical of invisible energy, surprisingly, he encouraged my exploration of Sukyo Mahikari. As an optical engineer, David tends to be more focused on the concrete than on the esoteric, yet he noticed early on the correlation between my spiritual practice of True Light and my allergic responses beginning to subside. When he would notice me getting stressed and coming down with allergies, he would sometimes ask "Have you received Light lately?" This would remind me to reach out to a Light giver to do so. Over time, his skepticism abated somewhat, as he could not deny the change he noticed in me. His engineering mindset caused him to test causation theories with an analytical approach. After much scrutiny, he was able to prove to his own satisfaction the connection between my well-being and receiving True Light.

After receiving Light for the first time, never again would I pursue the practice merely as a way to heal my allergies. I knew right away that there was a greater purpose. The conscious reconnection with the divine was so blissful that my first and most powerful impulse was to further pursue this reconnection. My next impulse was to learn how to offer this same gift to others. That would come soon enough! But first I would devote my efforts to receiving True Light as a way to begin to unite my life on spiritual and physical planes.

Roger Beck's Early Encounters with True Light

I've met some amazing True Light practitioners along the way, many of whom have become dear friends to me and my family. When I began to feel called to write a book about my experiences giving and receiving True Light, initially I thought I would just tell my own story. But when I talked with Roger Beck about it, I knew his story was also integral to this book. In fact, that encounter is a story in and of itself!

In Sukyo Mahikari there are professional groups in which people of similar backgrounds gather and form relationships of support and encouragement—educators' groups, health practitioners' groups, and scholars' groups, for example. I was invited to be part of the scholars' group, which was an interdisciplinary gathering available to serious practitioners where Roger was already a long-time member. The first time I went to the scholars' group, it was a small gathering of about eight or ten people. At one point I was sitting beside Roger and learned that he was an economist with a deeply profound practice of giving True Light. He had been practicing for quite some time at that point, whereas I was fairly new to the practice. As I sensed the depth and authenticity of his practice, I asked him how he was able to share the practice of giving True Light with his colleagues in his academic field—something I was eager to do. He responded quite matter-of-factly, "I have not been able to pass on my practice to any of my colleagues." This was astonishing to me. I could tell, having just met him, that Roger is one of the most pure souls on the planet. If he can't share the practice, how would I?

As I've gotten to know Roger quite well over the years, I have seen time and time again that he is indeed what I would call "a clear spring"— a person with an especially pure character. Many years ago he and I participated in a scholar's meeting in New York where I was speaking about self-reflection. I remember how quickly Roger engaged in an exercise in which I asked the group to call upon a childhood memory. Everyone engaged, but I remember vividly that Roger had immediate access to his own soul memories. This comes through as a joyous, childlike quality in him at times, which makes him very accessible as a scholar and quite endearing as a friend. I expected that his family and friends would see and admire this and want to at least borrow some of Roger's "divine spark" from him. But no. He told me that none of his family and friends had received the gift of giving True Light as a result of his example. Perhaps this was the moment that, unbeknownst to me, a seed was planted in my mind to share Roger's beautiful story through the book you now hold in your hands.

When I traveled to Japan to take an advanced Sukyo Mahikari course at the World Shrine Suza in Takayama in the Japanese Alps, Roger was there reviewing the course. After the course was complete, a large group of us traveled by bus to a very sacred Shinto shrine called Ise. Along the way, we stopped at the Sukyo Mahikari center where we were welcomed very warmly. People were paired up to give and receive True Light, and somehow, Roger and I were assigned to one another. As we gave each other Light, I recognized that this was part of a divine arrangement.

The Ise shrines are where the Japanese emperors receive covenants from God before a new reign begins. Toward the end of our time at Ise, we were taken to the sanctuary of the princess who had been given the responsibility of finding this sacred place by her father. Princess Yamatohime-no-mikoto's shrine was a beautiful forested area, which we walked through in deep serenity. As twilight fell and we were preparing to leave, I looked back at the gate of the princess' shrine and saw the setting sun streaming through in radiant beams. I wanted to capture the moment on film, but my camera was full. So I asked one of my traveling companions if she would be willing to take a photograph for me on her camera. She told me her camera was also full but, in a light-hearted way, she suggested we ask the princess for help. As she successfully snapped the photo, we both laughed and beamed at our good fortune. At that moment,

I noticed in the corner of my eye Roger smiling too. He had quietly observed us enjoying the natural beauty of this sacred space, with a genuine appreciation for the divine at play. When I noticed that Roger had smiled as he observed our wondrous experience, I was inspired to ask him to join me in writing about this beautiful spiritual path we share.

I asked Roger to begin by sharing with me his very first experience with receiving True Light. He responded by giving me a bit of his background story, beginning in the fall of 1979 when he was diagnosed with rheumatoid arthritis. Because he knew people who were badly impaired by arthritis, his diagnosis both shocked and frightened him. He was determined to do everything in his power to avoid the debilitating grasp of arthritis. Similar to my initial approach to my health issues, Roger's first step was to set up a medical team to help him manage this disease. But when all the medical community offered him was over-the-counter pain medication to treat the symptoms, which really didn't help at all, he began to explore non-pharmaceutical solutions by connecting with a wide variety of alternative health practitioners.

Over time, Roger experienced gradually worsening joint inflexibility, sometimes with mild pain, in his hands and feet. This gradual worsening was punctuated, every year or two, with severe but, thankfully, brief bouts of arthritic pain in other parts of his body. And, just as I had experienced, Roger told me that these widely spaced experiences with severe symptoms were always associated with unusual physical or emotional stress. Roger was especially good at tracking the cause and effect relationship between increased stress and increased pain. He noticed a pattern wherein within twenty-four hours of the stress experience, acute pain would follow. He told me about a time he had experienced intense arthritic pain in his shoulder within hours of dragging a boat across the sand to the water's edge. That amount of exertion was enough to trigger a major pain episode that might last up to a week.

As you can imagine, this caused Roger quite a bit of concern. He remained frightened by the possibility that his arthritis might ultimately bring him to a serious, painful, and debilitated condition. But rather than let his fear debilitate him, Roger used it to spark his intention to find a solution. For a period of about seven years, Roger engaged in an earnest, intent, wide-ranging, and open-minded search for a solution. He read widely and tried a variety of remedies including the Kelley Program (which emphasized detoxification), vitamin and mineral supplements, a macrobiotic diet and other dietary modifications, Transcendental Meditation, and herbal supplements. Nothing cured his arthritis—or even began to diminish it. While each of these remedies had solved an arthritis problem for others, none of them helped Roger. But what he did gain from this exhaustive study was an awakening to the critical importance of food quality in promoting health generally. Roger and I share this appreciation, and he has taken it to the point of growing much of his own food.

In August 1986, Roger took a trip to visit some friends in southeastern British Columbia, far from his Edmonton home. The day after he arrived, he experienced a massive arthritic attack—despite the absence of any extreme physical or emotional stress. He experienced severe inflammation in his right arm from wrist to elbow. Just moving his arm was intensely painful. He felt simply horrible from head to toe and spent the day in bed. When he told his friend about his extreme pain and suffering, his friend asked a simple question: "May I offer you True Light?" Roger knew his friend had become a member of Sukyo Mahikari, but he had no idea what that meant. Knowing Roger now, I'm not surprised to hear that he accepted his friend's offer, but Roger assures me that his positive response was surprising even to him at the time.

Before Roger's friend began to offer him True Light, he told Roger he needed to understand two things: "First and foremost, whatever happens is up to God, and second, I am not trying to cure you of any disease." Roger remembers his friend's words verbatim because he found these caveats so very unhelpful and incongruent with his worldview at the time. In his mind, his arthritis obviously needed a cure; that's why he was willing to receive True Light in the first place! But even more significant to Roger was the fact that he had been an atheist for more than twenty years. He didn't even believe in the God his friend claimed would control what would happen when he received True Light. Roger and I both laugh now as we reflect on how amazing it was that he was willing to receive True Light despite these troublesome "flaws" in his friend's thinking. But laughter aside, the truth is Roger was desperate for help. His fear of the effects arthritis might have on him was truly crippling.

Much to Roger's surprise, his friend radiated True Light from his hand to Roger's forehead, then to the back of his head and neck, and then to his lower back above the waist. He wondered why True Light was being directed to these parts of his body when the pain was in his arm. It would be some time before Roger came to understand the importance of purifying pain-free areas of the body in addition to painful areas. But even in that first time of receiving True Light, as his friend held his hand above his swollen arm, Roger felt a physical sensation unlike anything he had felt before. And he was amazed.

Roger recalls that the next morning he felt somewhat better. So that evening, when his friend offered to give him True Light again, he humbly accepted. His friend began by probing Roger's swollen arm, which felt like it was made of stone, with his fingertips. After his friend gave him True Light for about thirty minutes, Roger was surprised to find his arm had regained some degree of suppleness. By the next morning, Roger noticed further improvement in his overall condition. Somewhat stunned and speechless, Roger awkwardly thanked his friend for helping him in a way he could not begin to comprehend. As Roger prepared to head home, his friend told him how to contact someone in Edmonton in case he ever wanted to receive True Light again.

As if to underscore the difference between Roger's experience in British Columbia and his previous acute arthritic episodes, there was no improvement in his arm during the next three days when he did not receive True Light, even though historically his acute arthritic episodes normally reflected day-by-day improvement once past the peak of pain. Still not convinced that True Light was the cause of his relief, Roger couldn't deny that something inexplicable had happened when his friend had offered him that invisible gift.

About a week after he returned from British Columbia, Roger phoned his friend's Sukyo Mahikari contact in Edmonton, assuming that he would make arrangements to receive Light again in a few weeks. When he reached out to Dominique, who had established a temporary Sukyo Mahikari center in a house she rented not far from Roger's home in Edmonton, she was very persuasive in convincing him not to wait. So, a day or two later he arrived at the center. It was just a regular-looking suburban home in a middle class neighborhood, but even as Dominique welcomed him inside, he noticed that the house was sparkling clean. He could practically see his reflection in the dark gray tile floor in the vestibule.

Upon first meeting her, Dominique struck Roger as a strong person in every way. Roger guessed she was in her mid-thirties, and when he learned she taught ballet classes at a local dance studio, that explained her physical strength. But he also noted that she seemed strong in character as well—an all-around solid person. In a slightly French-sounding accent, Dominique welcomed Roger to the center and then immediately cautioned him that his goal of recovering from arthritis did not align with the purpose of receiving and giving Light. She could say nothing about whether there would be an impact on his physical condition. Rather, the purpose was spiritual purification which would allow him to grow closer to God—which, of course, Roger didn't believe in at the time. Discouraged by Dominique's insistence on the centrality of divine will, Roger weighed the benefits of what he had experienced in British

Columbia with his own desire for relief from pain and potential disability, and in so doing, allowed the scant possibility that giving True Light might actually have some spiritual significance. Clinging slightly less firmly to his atheism, but remaining fully committed to overcoming his arthritis, Roger concurred with Dominique that he would receive True Light in the way she had sincerely described it. Her dedication and expertise earned Roger's respect, even if he didn't agree with her belief in God.

When Dominique began to give Light, Roger was struck by the power of her practice. Her voice was loud and clear as she began to recite the prayer of purification. She was indeed a skilled Light practitioner, but because Dominique had dedicated her house as a temporary Sukyo Mahikari center, she was also practicing in a sacred space. Receiving True Light at a Sukyo Mahikari center would be a much more intense experience for Roger than receiving Light at his friend's house in British Columbia had been. He said it was physically unlike anything he had experienced up until that point in his life. He tried to describe the sensation he experienced while receiving True Light on his lower back, but he couldn't find any words other than "wonderful!" He said it was almost like he had entered an altered state of consciousness. Even though he still didn't know how he felt about spirituality, he kept coming back to the temporary Sukyo Mahikari center to receive True Light from Dominique two to three times per week.

By the end of September, Roger was still uncertain about Sukyo Mahikari and unable to fully wrap his mind around what was happening to him as he received True Light. But he felt that receiving True Light without being able to give True Light was too one-sided, so he asked if he could learn to give True Light—which would mean taking the primary spiritual development course. There was a primary course scheduled at the Sukyo Mahikari center in Seattle in mid-October, but to attend the primary course, Roger needed the approval of the person in charge of the Seattle Sukyo Mahikari Center. Looking back on this, Roger laughs at how unprepared he felt going into that telephone interview. His mind was still in turmoil with regard to his professed atheism and he really had no idea what he believed. But the Seattle director did not require him to accept any particular beliefs. Roger was welcomed to attend the primary course because his desire to give True Light to his family and others was grounded in pure altruism.

Roger was attentive throughout the three-day primary spiritual development course, but he now admits, at the time, he really didn't feel as though he had absorbed much or achieved much clarity of mind from listening to the teachings. But on the third day, when he received his omitama—the divine pendant that allows practitioners to give True Light, something shifted in Roger. Metaphorically, an omitama is like a magnifying glass that concentrates the sun's rays—except it concentrates God's True Light. In physical form, the omitama is a small, circular golden locket which hangs on a chain and is placed in a white cloth pocket sewn inside a practitioner's undergarment. It is handled with reverence and clean hands each time it is put on or taken off. The spiritual leader of Sukyo Mahikari creates an omitama for each practitioner so each person's omitama is their own. Having an omitama connected Roger to God by a spiritual cord, allowing him to radiate True Light, despite any impurities he may have accumulated over many lifetimes.

By the time Roger completed the primary course, he no longer identified as an atheist. Looking back on his visit with his friends in August of 1986, Roger once told me with tears in his eyes "I can see how God reached down, picked me up, and turned me around 180 degrees" as he described his introduction to Sukyo Mahikari as the loving redirection of his life.

You will notice throughout this book that we often use the verb "to allow" when describing events, large and small, in our life stories. This is quite intentional, as it reflects a humble acceptance that even while we are thoroughly engaged and active in our lives, we acknowledge the divine arrangements by which all things are allowed to transpire. With this awareness, we begin to partner with God in working toward transformation of self and the world, with God as a loving companion guiding all things toward the good of all.

The primary spiritual development course teaches that if we practice giving and receiving True Light we will gradually come to understand the divine principles behind and within the experience. But we also have spiritual experiences that help us gain wisdom. Roger went to the center and gave and received True Light two to three times a week and began giving True Light at his home. He had many spiritual experiences as he gave True Light that could not be explained within normal sensory-based thinking. Roger told me of a time when giving True Light alleviated his wife's extreme pain. She was rolling from side to side in bed, clutching her sides in an unexplained agony, so Roger offered her True Light. After several minutes of receiving Light her pain disappeared completely. Roger was dumbfounded. Yet he continued to give and receive True Light even though he did not understand it.

Roger was amazed to find that, mysteriously, the prediction that he would come to understand the divine or universal principles through giving and receiving True Light (and further study of the principles) proved to be correct. As he made spiritual progress, concepts he had been conscious of but did not understand suddenly became clear to him, one after another.

After two years, Roger attended the secondary spiritual development course. Although he was still hoping for a cure to his arthritis, he was no longer frightened by it. He was able to leave the question of his arthritis in God's hands and accept whatever outcome God arranged. After another two or three years, his arthritis symptoms simply disappeared. He was deeply moved by this change, which filled him with a profound gratitude that fuels his desire to repay God for this great blessing.

The Purification Process Continues

I'm so grateful to have heard Roger's story from the beginning. Having met him long after his early years in Sukyo Mahikari, it would be easy for me to falsely assume that Roger always had the profound gratitude he now radiates and that the beginning of his spiritual journey was just as natural for him as it appears to be now. I appreciate his willingness to be transparent and even a bit vulnerable in sharing how he began to incorporate spiritual practice into his everyday life even while he remained an atheist. It causes me to reflect on my own beginnings with the same deep humility and effusive gratitude Roger embodies.

Roger and I both initially entered into the spiritual practice of receiving True Light because we suffered physical maladies. But, as I mentioned previously, immediately after my first time of receiving True Light I knew there was much more to the experience than improved physical health. Awakened to the deeper spiritual dimension of the practice, I continued to receive Light and developed a strong desire to give others Light by a pure soul motivation and not to derive any specific benefit.

First I started purifying my home by giving it True Light. Then I began to radiate True Light as part of the process of preparing my family's meals. I have always cooked for my family by my own hand as much as possible and now I am humbled to enjoy the fine, inspired cooking my daughter Mira does regularly. As a child, I enjoyed hand-cooked daily meals that made me feel deeply at home and happy. I realized that the food my family prepared was not only fresh and organic, but also filled with love and wisdom imparted by those who prepared the food because they invested themselves in its preparation. I was given a model of a daily food preparation practice embodying a spiritual dimension through which love and wisdom were transferred across the generations. This model remains alive within me today and I build upon it by filling the food with Light and gratitude, spreading the vibrations of harmony with God and nature. I feel happy and fulfilled each time I can give and nurture in this way or in other very simple day to day ways such as making a bed beautifully, purifying a room with Light, making it clean and tidy for someone's use or enjoyment and teaching others to do this to express gratitude and to care, love and nurture in small, daily ways.

Food preparation is an especially sacred time. As a first step, after grocery shopping one of my family members or I give True Light to groceries for twenty minutes. I also cook with one hand raised over the pot to further purify and fill the food with True Light. I feel wonderful harmony and deep gratitude for this food preparation process, especially as I serve this food to my family. After following these practices for about a year, I decided to launch an experiment to see if the practice of True Light had had any impact on my food allergies. I had been allergic to eggs, peanuts, soybeans, and carrots for many years. I tried eating small quantities of each food one by one. No reactivity, no allergies!

Regular bouts of hay fever and sinusitis also disappeared from my life. Once in a while, say, once in a few years, I experience a few sneezes but I've not been debilitated by my seasonal or food allergies since I began giving True Light. I have learned to think of these few sneezes as a way to eliminate some impurities, so I offer gratitude for that blessing. Similarly, I give and receive True Light bearing in mind that what is often thought to be illness is actually a cleansing of the spirit, mind, and body.

I have come to understand this process of cleansing the toxins from my system and the ensuing elimination of some of my accumulated spiritual, mental, and physical impurities to be a reflection of God's great love for me. Ultimately, it seems, this arrangement has been established to promote our greater health, harmony, and prosperity. As I give and receive True Light during such a cleansing, I experience this truth clearly and my gratitude deepens. Over time, these experiences have helped me to overcome the misunderstanding that cleansing phenomena are illnesses. Thus my inner attitude and verbal responses to cleansing in others and myself is deeply grateful and positive in place of what they used to be. Common expressions of sympathy "I am so sorry," or disheartenment, "I feel so bad or tired..." are naturally replaced by a smile filled with gratitude. Thanks to receiving and giving True Light with gratitude for the cleansing, plus apology for my impurities, I usually overcome the cleansing within a few hours or days. I become fully revived, positive, and hopeful. Although I do accept that I may need to take medication when cleansing, I have not had to take any allergy medications since I began giving True Light in 2002.

But it wasn't that simple. As my sinusitis and food allergies began to subside, a series of very severe skin allergies and eczema, manifesting as swelling of the skin on my hands and arms, began to erupt. My skin oozed fluid and blood. It itched so intensely I couldn't resist scratching. But even in my discomfort, deep inside, my innermost consciousness was grateful and accepting of these phenomena as cleansings.

My change in attitude may have been even more significant than the physical changes I was experiencing. Although in the past I had been patient with suffering, by sincerely giving and receiving True Light I became grateful, positive, and strong inside. Whenever someone asked how I was, the words and tone of my response resounded with positivity. And, as I reflected on my experiences, I realized I was becoming stronger, healthier, and more vital. I was filled with a sense of calm.

Throughout this entire process, I combined the art of True Light with medical advice. Sometimes people around me were overwhelmed and distressed at the sight of my hands and arms, wanting me to adopt different medical interventions to cure the eczema and interrupt the oozing. But I knew that would have suppressed the elimination of toxins, so I remained centered through these experiences, grasping the truth of my cleansing with gratitude, acceptance, and apology for my part and on behalf of my ancestors. Thus, I found the strength to bear my own pain, to understand the pain it brought to those watching, and communicate with them empathically while continuing to focus on confidently giving and receiving True Light.

I also received guidance and learned that skin cleansings discharge old and dangerous toxins accumulated over time, possibly passed down over generations. Discharge from the skin prevents these toxins from accumulating in vital organs and causing more serious illnesses. I was grateful to learn this and could grasp the truth in the guidance. It was a felt experience and my gratitude for my long-term health and well-being soared. This guidance allowed me to go through my skin cleansings more easily and confidently. Giving and receiving True Light always alleviated the pain and discomfort from my skin cleansings. The extra effort made to give True Light at such times—when it would have been much easier to just receive Light—helped me to engage in my own transformation. I saw myself as more quickly refreshed and more quickly experiencing positive change.

My background in psychology and my experience as a professor of psychology facilitated my capacity to reflect more deeply as I went through these experiences, and in so doing I was able to further cultivate my reflective mind. I actively pondered the spiritual meaning of my experiences as I gave and received True Light. For instance, one day as I was receiving True Light I realized that I was being allowed to eliminate some of the toxic medicines accumulated in my body since childhood. The taste in my mouth at that moment matched the remembered taste of the medicines I was given as child. It was a truly amazing experience, and one that I know others have experienced as well. My gratitude and desire to give True Light continually increased. After two or three years of giving and receiving True Light, my intense skin cleansings ceased, and have not returned.

But there was another layer of healing yet to come. As a young girl, I was found to have an underactive thyroid gland and was medicated with iodine. My thyroid normalized until, as an adult, I experienced Hashimoto's thyroiditis, an autoimmune condition where the immune system attacks the thyroid gland. My internist referred me to an endocrinologist who ran various tests.

As I awaited the results, I reflected and realized once again that all cleansings are truly for the better. I had overcome my previous ailments, and now I began to see health issues not as mere illnesses, but as cleansings of physical, mental, and spiritual impurities. I was able to recognize that I was actually being blessed with the opportunity to further strengthen my spirit, mind, and body by meeting the challenge of Hashimoto's thyroiditis.

This realization centered me and gave me confidence that everything would eventually work out well. I decided that my primary response to this diagnosis would be to practice True Light with joy, love, and sincerity. I would also follow my doctor's guidance, while continuing to lead a balanced, healthy life. My felt connection to God strengthened as I focused on giving True Light at the Sukyo Mahikari center and at home with more love and sincerity.

But, as with my previous health issues, I continued to consult with my medical doctors. I had a battery of tests every six months, followed by a meeting with the endocrinologist. While I was aware of the spiritual dimension of my process at my medical appointments, I was also keenly aware that my endocrinologist was not. I often thought about sharing my spiritual practice of True Light with him, but as soon as the thought would enter my mind, he would make some remark praising the rigor of his scientific education while pointing to his dismissal of holistic health practices. Finally, when I could no longer resist explaining something about my approach, his only response was a blank stare. Here's how it unfolded:

Dr. E: *I may eventually need to start you on Synthroid. You've been managing your Hashimoto's amazingly well so far, but I don't want you be disappointed if it catches up with you.*

Me: *I hope not. I try not to take medicines unless absolutely necessary.*

Dr. E: *Well you've been lucky, so far. But medication is usually required, eventually. Diet alone won't solve the problem.*

Me: *Well, in addition to choosing healthy organically grown food, I actually bless the food before and during meal preparation. The food itself carries the blessing to my body.*

Dr. E: *(awkward silence)*

Me: *I've been giving and receiving spiritual blessings called True Light. These blessings are given directly to my body as well. I think this has contributed significantly to my well-being.*

Dr. E: *(sustained blank stare)*

My endocrinologist saw me over an eight-year period, during which he considered prescribing medications a few times—but always chose instead to monitor my condition a little while longer. In hindsight, I realize I was effectively combining the art of True Light with medical treatment in a process closely calibrated by unseen divine hands. I could feel the profound love of God permeating the process of restoring my health and well-being through means that preserved the integrity of my spiritual and physical bodies. This process, I perceive, was true medicine, the slow, deep, complete process of restoration to health and well-being through relationships. There was great care in the relationships, unseen and seen. Health was being restored without doing harm and with great care—a high, patient, committed form of care.

The last time I saw my endocrinologist, he reviewed my test results as usual, then said "I'd love to keep seeing you, but there is no reason to anymore." My Hashimoto's thyroiditis had resolved to his satisfaction and he was ready to write a report to my internist. He spoke with me with heartfelt openness at my final appointment, saying he was in considerable pain himself due to conditions of his own. I returned home wondering how I could effectively share True Light with him. I decided to speak with another practitioner of True Light who is a physician. I asked if he would be willing to meet and give True Light to my endocrinologist. His response was enthusiastic, so I wrote a long letter of thanks to my endocrinologist, described the art of True Light, and invited him to meet me and a friend of mine (who is also a physician) at the Sukyo Mahikari center to receive True Light. There was no response.

I pray that this kind soul, who responded to me with such patience and non-invasiveness, will someday be open to receiving True Light himself and practice true medicine in harmony with universal principles.

Of course, my family witnessed all of this over time. Although they winced at my skin lesions and wished for my sake the Hashimoto's thyroiditis would abate, they respected my wishes for the higher harmony these phenomena offered me. And they supported my commitment to giving and receiving True Light. My gratitude to them grew deeper and deeper and remains with me as I thank God for the restoration of my health.

Sharing True Light with Others

I will never forget the day my daughter Mira asked to come with me to the Sukyo Mahikari Los Angeles Center to receive True Light and participate in the sacred monthly thanksgiving ceremony. She was only about ten or eleven years old at the time when one night she said "Mom, I'm going to come with you tomorrow." So she woke before dawn on a Sunday morning and cheerfully hopped in the car as the sun began to peek over the horizon. I remember feeling especially happy as we made our way to the center and in a moment of high vibration I asked her if she wanted to learn to give Light. She said, "Yes I want to give Light to Nolan and Kira," who were two little children of long-time Sukyo Mahikari practitioners at the Pasadena Center. Her words and her wish to give Light with me filled me with joy as I imagined the great gifts this spiritual practice would bring her over her lifetime.

I was with Mira when she received her holy omitama. It was a special time for our very special bond, which coincided with an omitama accident on my part. The omitama, when taken off one's body, must be held above one's navel at all times and must not be placed even in its own omitama box in any place that a person may sit or the lower part of the body may touch, such as on a bed or a car seat. During Mira's primary course, on the last morning as I was getting dressed for the day, I accidentally placed my omitama in its box on my bed. I realized my mistake almost immediately and upon reaching the center reported this to staff. With a deep prayer of gratitude for my holy omitama and for my daughter being allowed to receive her holy omitama, apology for my deep spiritual impurities and a material offering, I gave my omitama for purification. When I received my purified omitama, its preciousness to me in my daily life was heightened. Mira learned the prayer of purification and began giving Light at the Pasadena Center with me and at home.

One year later, my son Rudy took the primary Sukyo Mahikari course, received holy omitama, and began giving True Light, followed by my husband David a couple of years later and my sister Shouma in India. Then four years after that, my son Ives and Santanov, Rudy's friend and collaborator in their solar energy business who has become part of our family. In parallel, during these years a total of eighteen colleagues, friends, and my children's friends—some with close family members, a mother, a daughter and husbands, also received the primary course to receive omitama to give Light. Through inviting closely connected people to receive Light at home and at centers, one by one my family and friends had spiritual experiences of their own and chose to incorporate this spiritual practice into their lives.

It gives me great joy to see my family and friends engaged in this humble yet miraculous practice based entirely in the giving and receiving of God's most loving Light and, gradually but steadily, awakening to harmony with the divine principles in the universe in their daily lives. From my earliest experiences with True Light, my desire has been to share this practice with others. That's why I was so surprised to learn from Roger that his family and colleagues had not joined him in this practice that causes him to simply radiate God's love. Had the people around him not seen the pure goodness that he exudes? Were they intimidated by the depth of his practice? I can't be sure, but I'm inspired to share more of his story with you, dear reader, in the hope that you will relate to the way this deeply generous spiritual man contributes to true harmony in the world through his daily practice.

Our Spiritual Roots

Sometimes I have to remind myself that Roger wasn't always a person devoted to spiritual practice. He called himself an atheist for twenty years. When I asked him about his years as a devout atheist, the broad smile on his face revealed even greater incredulity than that which fueled my curiosity. Looking back, he recognizes how much evidence he chose to ignore in order to maintain two decades of unbelief.

Roger was raised in a Christian family. His father was Christian Scientist, but throughout childhood, Roger and his brother attended mass at the Episcopal church to which their mother belonged. He learned the basics of the faith and received confirmation, but never really grasped it all. He told me a story about asking his parents about the concept of the Trinity. "How could something be three things and at the same time be only one thing?" he asked, but never received an explanation that made sense to him. This likely was an early indication that Roger's intellect would need special attention to extend comprehension beyond the physical dimension. His maternal grandfather was an exceptional stained glass artist and craftsman, so that was one more religious influence in his life, while his paternal grandmother was a very devout Christian Scientist who ran the Christian Science reading room in his hometown. But after graduating high school first in his class, Roger matriculated at MIT, where he distanced himself from his Christian roots and embraced an atheistic mindset.

Roger humbly informed me he was not the smartest student in his high school, but earned valedictorian status because he was able to earn top grades in spite of his academic shortcomings. That would not be easy to repeat in college. In fact, MIT probably wasn't the best fit for Roger, as he struggled mightily with his chemistry and physics courses. They say being an undergraduate at MIT is like trying to drink water from a fire hose. Roger would agree! But he made it through the heavy science and engineering requirements with the help of a tutor arranged for him by his fraternity brothers and eventually found his strengths in MIT's Industrial Management program.

The sense of responsibility Roger gained by being part of a self-managed fraternity and the humility gained by being in over his head academically probably served Roger best at MIT. By the time he graduated, he had read Ayn Rand's *Atlas Shrugged*. Her case for atheism was combined with a political and economic utopian view that resonated strongly with Roger. And so, he bought the whole package. Looking back, Roger says he was a prime candidate for atheism because he not only had an intellectual bent, he had a strong personal ego that gave rise to the mistaken notion that there is nothing in this world higher than human beings. It would take an encounter with the divine to set him free of that mindset.

My initial experience with True Light may have been less of a reach for me, as it reminded me of the many divine encounters I had experienced as a child growing up in India. As Eiko gave me True Light for the very first time at Lorri's office, I recognized an immediate profound connection with the infinite. It was an experience of coming alive to the depths of truth, love, and harmony within and it was powerful! I felt serene, calm, and incredulous.

I had felt direct connection with the infinite as a child, particularly when I spent summers at my maternal grandparents' home in Santiniketan in the Bengal countryside in India. My grandparents had made this place their retirement home among a community of extraordinary people. In my grandparents' presence, as well as in other places where members of my family—particularly my elders—gathered, I often had profound feelings of connection and happiness. Remembering those times fills my heart with an indescribable warmth I've come to know so well.

Memories of Santiniketan are especially vivid. Now a university town that attracts tourists from all around the world, Santiniketan was founded and developed by members of the Tagore family in the late 19th century. According to lore, Debendranath Tagore—a philosopher who was both one of the key figures in the Bengali Renaissance and the father of the famous poet, playwright, and composer Rabindranath Tagore—was taking a boat ride when he became captivated by the beauty of the chhatim trees and palm groves that offered him shade and a perfect place for meditation. He bought a large tract of land there, planted some saplings, and built a small guest house which he called his "abode of peace" or Santiniketan. His son Rabindranath later composed this poem to describe the place:

She is our own, the darling of our hearts, Santiniketan.

In the shadows of her trees we meet

in the freedom of her open sky.

Our dreams are rocked in her arms.

Her face is a fresh wonder of love every time we see her,

for she is our own, the darling of our hearts.

— *Rabindranath Tagore*, [17]

In 1901, Rabindranath Tagore founded an experimental school, and later a university at Santiniketan, where children and students received their lessons seated on mats under the canopy of trees so they could learn in the tradition of the ancient forest hermitages. Tagore wrote many of his world famous poems in this holy ashram and went on to win the Nobel Prize in Literature in 1913. I was blessed to have spent a portion of my childhood in this sacred place.

My connection to Santiniketan was very strong even as my father's military career demanded that he move us as a family every few years. These moves, buffered by the warmth of family, the larger military family, and cantonment life, gave me resilience and courage as we went through wars and witnessed the selflessness of military personnel close to us in the defence of country. My grandparents' home, in contrast, was a serene, unchanging summer sanctuary for me. Their Hindu faith took root in the same fertile land not far from that which had attracted Debendranath Tagore to the shores of the Kopai River. "I have the nonattachment of a bird," my maternal grandfather used to say of himself. I internalized the vibration and meaning of his words, which come alive in me to this day in the context of giving and receiving Light. As Rabindranath Tagore wrote in his signature style, "Beyond a distant river somewhere, in the edge of a thick forest…you're finding your way." Indeed, I began my journey there, with fireflies punctuating many fond memories of watching the heat of the day rise from the red soil into the starry night sky.

I wonder about your early experiences with God, dear reader. Does the smell and sight of the simple white candles adorning your dinner table sometimes transport you back to your days as a young acolyte? Does a certain strain of melody played on a clarinet remind you of the many bar and bat mitzvahs you attended in your youth? Did you have a mitzvah yourself? Did you take comfort in the rituals performed each Sunday at churches like the one to which Roger and his brother accompanied their mother? Or do you find greater comfort under the tall trees as Tagore did? Do you keep a statue of the Buddha in your home as a tribute to your ancestors? Or, like me, do you have a grandparent whose life of nonattachment freed you to consider such a life for yourself?

As we continue this journey together of exploring what it means to integrate spiritual practice into our daily lives, I encourage you to bring your memories and experiences with you. Bring your whole self, whether that includes a specific faith or a vision on the future's distant horizon only you can see. The spiritual life is a journey that starts somewhere for everyone. Thank you for allowing me to share with you some of my earliest experiences with giving and receiving True Light. I'm humbled to share Roger's stories with you as well, as his commitment to spiritual practice has inspired me for many years.

The stories we claim as our own might just tell us more about the future than they can tell us about the past. I hope you will give yourself the gift of taking some time to reflect on your own stories. Have you witnessed miracles? How do you approach life's mysteries? Have you experienced moments of clarity amidst the chaos of uncertainty of modern life? Have you ever had a direct encounter with the divine? Are you devoted to truth seeking through science and empirical knowledge? Are you open to what may be? What is your story? I'd love to hear you tell it.

I've invited several esteemed colleagues, friends, and family to share brief reflections in the "spotlights" section following each chapter. I'm very grateful to them for bringing such rich insight and experience to the pages of this book. I wonder if you'd like to take a few moments after reading the spotlights to write, perhaps in your personal journal, your own reflections on each chapter. As I mentioned in the preface, "Your spirit, your mind, and your body are just as important to this book as are the spirits, minds, and bodies of the people who have contributed to its content. Please consider yourself an integral part of this compilation, in which your personal stories are welcome alongside those you are reading." I eagerly invite you to join us on the journey!

Chapter 1

Spotlights

Amaranta Nehru

There is something between the words in this chapter that moves me and reminds me of my true self. There is a sense of strong power and connection that is more than simple resonance. I am almost able to hear the sound of a gentle voice reading the lines out. It seems this writing doesn't come from the mind but from the soul, as it has the effect of being mysteriously moving. I am grateful to be reminded of rich and soulful experiences from my own life that seem to have been buried. I feel a sense of revival of the most important in my encounter with these words; reminding me of who I really am and why I am here. The part about Santiniketan reminded me of the one time I visited there nineteen years ago. Aboard the train from Kolkata, I encountered a baul singer whose mystical music moved me with its power. I'm reminded of the end of the film "Spirited Away" by Studio Ghibli when the boy, Haku, is released from the spell of the witch when the girl, Chichiro, reminds him of his real name. Such is the powerful effect of reminding people of who they are. And to me these words have this kind of an effect.

Lanette Darby, PhD

This chapter extends a clear, heartwarming, and honest invitation to a journey that awakens our soul-self and spiritual knowingness. The insightful accounts that describe the profound experiences of giving and receiving True Light direct us to knowing our true self and the underlying spiritual foundation that all humans share with one another. In "climbing up the mountain of daily living" in the uncertainty and chaos of modern life this chapter offers a respite of insight and wisdom. Thank you for taking us on a journey that integrates our spiritual, mental, and physical lives, thus directing us on a path of true happiness.

Gail Breakey, MPH

Receiving and giving True Light, especially at the dojo (Sukyo Mahikari center), provides a deep sense of peace and lifts one up in understanding of God and truth. The challenge is to incorporate this sense of inspiration into our daily life for continuity. This can be achieved by giving and receiving Light and also by receiving inspiration from the Prayer Book and Holy book. This is critically important as we must become "purified" to participate in the transformation of our civilization, currently undergoing traumatic upheaval, into a more just, spirit-oriented world as requested by God through the founder of Sukyo Mahikari.

John Cobb, PhD

I, for one, have no doubt that Sukyo Mahikari has helped many people, and that those who are helped often seek to help others. We can all rejoice! I am myself grateful that my daughter-in-law, Kimi Cobb (Director of the Pasadena

Sukyo Mahikari Center), has gone to great trouble to give me Light. I always feel better, but some might say that is because of relaxing for much longer than I might otherwise, while also enjoying Kimi's presence. However, one time it seemed to be much more for me. For some months I had been feeling my age (ninety-five) and dragging myself around. One morning, shortly after Kimi gave me Light, I woke up rejuvenated. Coincidence? Who can say? I prefer to credit the True Light.

Chapter 2

Elevation of the Mind

hen we decide to embark on the spiritual journey—and when we commit to the daily practices, disciplines, and studies that cultivate a spiritual way of living—we begin to notice things we had not noticed before. Our minds become attuned to the subtle energies that make up the universe and we perceive meaning more clearly, both in interactions and events. As our perception and understanding changes and elevates, we begin to change how we live. In Sukyo Mahikari, the spirit-mind-body connection represents a chain reaction of sorts, where our spiritual transformation impacts mind and body and the world around us as well.

Early in my spiritual practice, while receiving True Light from a Sukyo Mahikari staff member, I had an experience that changed my life. I was receiving True Light to my main soul, directed toward the center of my forehead, when I was allowed to see—in the deepest depths of myself—the round, radiant, still, golden circle of energy which I recognized instantly as my divine soul. The awe, humility, and serenity I felt for being allowed to receive this direct experience of true self is beyond my capacity to put into words. For in that precious moment

I realized that this serene, pure, luminous human core is universal, equal across people of all external differences of circumstance, history, and qualities. It can be seen and felt through direct experience by an ordinary human being like me, living an ordinary life within the ordinary environment of family and professional life. The self-awareness that accompanied the gift of seeing my divine soul left an indelible mark on my consciousness. I became fully and completely aware that my essence or true self is divine energy connected with God and all existence.

Another unforgettable experience that occurred early in my spiritual practice also left me forever changed. In my professional capacity as a professor of clinical psychology, I was leading a group of psychotherapists in reflective dialogue to develop self-awareness. Following the spiritual guidance I received, these reflective meetings began taking place in more personal settings, beginning with my home and later rotating through other group members' homes. The work was just as professional and organized as before, but people were more open, warm and relational in the home setting.

At one such meeting, it so happened that I was sitting with my back to a picture window as I spoke to the group. It was late May and there was a tulip tree in bloom outside. The group was sitting facing me, with a lovely view of the tree through the window. As I shared psychological reflections I decided to go deeper to share spiritual reflections as well. It took some courage on my part, but I decided to go deeper and share from my personal spiritual experience. I could feel the group was very moved to hear what I had to say. There was a warmth in the room and a long silence following my talk. Then someone spoke up and said that the whole time I was speaking, the tulip tree outside shed petals like a rain shower and when I stopped speaking the shower of petals stopped as well. Everyone else simply nodded their heads. We all shared a sense of awe, a sense that we had experienced greatness, something extraordinary intertwined with the ordinary in our everyday lives. No more words were needed. There was a mysterious, undeniable, and logically inexplicable harmony between nature and the words I spoke. It moved me deeply to know that as I spoke nature responded and participated, thus helping everyone in the room to experience this harmony and open their hearts to listen to their true selves. It was a powerful experience. Such is the depth of experience I have been allowed to have and share with others in the journey of developing the reflective mind through the spiritual practice of the art of True Light.

Deciding to approach our time on earth as a spiritual journey is a decision to embrace transformation over time. But some things do change immediately. Giving and receiving True Light is a transformative practice that shifts both giver and receiver away from material-centeredness toward spirit-centeredness. Very early in my spiritual journey, I was given very clear insight into the importance of tending to spirit, mind, and body—in that order. In his book *God's Light and Universal Principals for all Humanity*, Sydney Chang defines "spirit-first" as giving "priority to spiritual values and to consider all things in light of God's will." Over time I have realized that many of my purifications—which can appear in the form of physical, emotional, relational, financial, and other types of challenges—have been for my mind to elevate and discern God's will. This infusion of spirituality into every aspect of daily life and the embrace of divine will is my emphasis in the book you now hold in your hands, and so, the theme of spirituality will be a common thread throughout its chapters. But, as we go deeper into the spiritual transformation at the heart of the journey, I'd like to invite you to explore with me the transformation of mind as an integral part of the process.

What Is the Mind?

As a professor of psychology, I devoted much of my career to working with neglected and abused children from disadvantaged families and very often families of color, as well as with teams of psychologists with similar caseloads. I've been blessed to work with some amazing clinicians along the way. The depth of commitment, breadth of knowledge, and skillful means I have seen has been truly amazing. I have witnessed over and over, in countless cases, the miraculous resiliency of the human mind. And yet, most of the clinicians I've worked with would have difficulty stating a concise and meaningful definition for the word "mind." Some connect the mind primarily with the brain, while others have a more abstract understanding of the psyche, but across the discipline of psychology there really is no good definition of the mind, as my colleague and friend Dr. Dan Siegel has insightfully observed. Dan is a faculty member at UCLA School of Medicine, as well as founding co-director of the Mindful Awareness Research Center at UCLA and executive director of the Mindsight Institute, which links science, clinical practice, education, the arts, and contemplation. Through an interdisciplinary process, he arrived at an expansive definition of the mind as "the flow of energy and information within a person and between people." This non-physical understanding of the mind is nonetheless very connected to the brain, which in accordance with the leading edge of brain science, Dan locates in the head, the heart, and the gut.

I've been very fortunate to work with Dan Siegel in a number of capacities. I first met him after I received the primary course for Light giving, when a former student of mine suggested I join Dan's study circles in Los Angeles. His first book, *The Developing Mind,* had been published and he was beginning to establish the field of Interpersonal Neurobiology (IPNB.) I found his book very interesting and had begun sharing it in my graduate-level family therapy classrooms. This was the book that later led to Dan being invited to the Vatican by Pope John Paul II, who wanted to better understand why the fact that his mother had looked into his eyes when he was an infant was so important to his lifelong mental health. Even with all the excitement surrounding his book, Dan responded to my first email with an enthusiastic welcome to his study circle.

The group was warm and inviting. I felt comfortable with everyone, including Dan. At one point I found myself saying something about the need for a new type of research to capture the kind of work going on in the study circle. The group wanted to hear more, so they urged Dan and me to sit in the center of the group's circle and talk with each other about this. We both agreed to this "fishbowl" arrangement, but when Dan asked me what kind of research it would be I completely froze. I could neither think nor speak. I experienced total overwhelm. My mind was blocked. I felt deep pain in my brain. The group commented that I was emotionally flooded, meaning stress from unresolved trauma in my brainstem was flooding my brain and overriding thoughts and words. I felt the tension and deep pain in the left side of my head, traveling down to my neck and shoulder. All I could feel was terror. It was extremely painful and yet I was in the best place I could be for such an intense experience, as Dan was deeply present with me. I realized he was listening deeply to my true self beneath the trauma when he said "Some things are so deep there are no words for them." That was all he said, but the truth in his words caused serenity and peace to well up deep within me. We sat together with the group in silence for a short time. I felt that our colleagues in the circle honored the truth in our exchange and together, all of us, if only for a short time, tapped into the silence of a realm deeper than the mind—the realm of soul or true self.

Now, sixteen years later during the COVID-19 pandemic, I recently came upon the work of a prescient interdisciplinary scientist Mary Helen Immordino-Yang and her colleagues in Dan Siegel's PEPP MWE UP online gathering. Their work reveals that the brainstem, which contains the basic mechanisms to keep us alive on the physical plane, is also the part of the brain that is activated when we have deep experiences such as awe and inspiration. It shows that capacities for basic physical survival and highest connection are very old in human beings.[7] This kind of research that combines reflective narrative and physical measurement of psychophysiology and neuroimaging may be the kind of research that will one day study our whole self—spirit, mind, and body—our highest capacities for relationship, and our deepest capacities for reflection. By highest capacity for relationship I mean our capacity for relationship with God, with our own souls, and with the souls of others. By our deepest capacity for reflection I mean our capacity to reflect on the divine wisdom transmitted through these deep inner relationships, as well as the capacity to self realize and become fully self aware. To conduct such work, scientists and those who develop new scientific technologies and instrumentation will themselves need to purify and elevate their spirits, minds, and bodies. At a time when such connection between divine wisdom and science is allowed, I can imagine the depth of humility in human beings and the harmony in society that will emerge. I hope such a time is near and colleagues can prepare for it by purifying souls together and elevating minds with True Light to create a culture in which the divine wisdom is spoken. I pray that we may have the words for it and understand each other as we speak, discerning its profundity and significance for daily life and scientific inquiry.

Perhaps the field of psychology dovetails with the mind/spirit connection more easily than most, but in my experience, anyone who acknowledges Spirit in their workplace may experience these windows of pure awareness as I have throughout the course of my career. A similar experience of unexpectedly sharing silence with colleagues took place at my Monday morning faculty meeting at Alliant International University, where I was serving as a professor of clinical psychology. We were going around the room sharing life updates when I decided to share my spiritual practice of giving Light. I recall that there was pin-drop silence in response. A reverent silence, though silence nonetheless among colleagues. Our hearts may have united with the Infinite in that moment, though I cannot say if this was so for our conscious minds. Such experiences in my professional life have given me a taste of the possibility of the elevation of the mind in connected relationships wherever we are—in our families, workplaces, and communities.

At the time of that first study class with Dan, I had just received my holy omitama and I was already beginning to disengage from the dominant state of the scientific paradigm as I became more interested in its evolution. Actually, I had felt all along that something fundamental was missing in the foundations of knowledge—especially in higher education—and that the pedagogy needed to become more experiential, subjective, and deeply personal. As I deepened my spiritual practice, I began to see that the missing element in education is the Light of divine wisdom. I was lucky to have been nurtured closer to it in my childhood in India, but the lifetime process of formalized education had whittled away divine wisdom in exchange for mere human knowledge.

A few years later in 2013, as I was beginning to form a similar group of circles, I went back to Dan's colloquium for a year. During one of the sessions, I decided to share about my Light giving practice, which sparked his interest. Subsequently, I met Dan one-on-one and offered Light to his main soul, which is seated between the eyes in the place some refer to as the "third eye." I remember his pure and humble response: "That was very nice, though I do not know what it is." At my invitation, most of the people in the colloquium group came to the Sukyo Mahikari Los Angeles Center for an introductory talk from two Sukyo Mahikari staff members and a full session of Light. Dan responded by thanking me for the invitation and said he will come at another time.

Spirituality, Science, and Society

The intersection of the mind and spirit is a topic drawing more people from across disciplines and traditions. The study of psychology—really all sciences— is incomplete without awareness of the spiritual element of all people and all of creation. Spiritual and religious traditions recognize the importance of the mind in the journey of faith now more than ever. Soon it will be time for mind and spirit to arrive at full integration. This will begin to happen as we cultivate the elevation of our minds to see through our spiritual eyes. This point of integration is the convergence of personal and impersonal truth seen by a human being then proven empirically. For the subjective (personal and usually unseen) and the objective (impersonal and usually seen) aspects of truth to converge in human perception, human lives must harmonize with God and the universal principles in daily life. For meaning to be seen as clearly as a concrete object, and in the same or similar way by many observers, deep spiritual impurities common to humanity, the spiritual pollution of the soul must be wiped away from the vibrations of the innermost attitude. Then the torchlight of divinity and divine wisdom in every soul that comes from our connection with God can shine through the mind. The mind can elevate to know and be in harmony with the will of God. As we begin to develop this capacity to discern and grow with the will of God, then we begin to become instruments of convergence and full integration of the spirit and mind, and thus naturally of the spirit, mind, and body.

True spiritual practices in daily life that can give people, families, and, through them, fields of human endeavor (including the sciences) the chance to elevate in spirit, mind, and body will allow people to begin reclaiming true humanity, discerning the will of God, transforming and elevating the paradigm of knowledge to integrate personal and impersonal truth seen through spiritual eyes and recognized as God's divine will. This harmony with God and the universal principles deep within the human being as it begins to be cultivated widely in the world will be the beginning of the divine wisdom uniting with human wisdom and divine science with human science. To receive such conditions of elevation, we as a human family must elevate to be in harmony with Light through true spiritual practice in daily life.

One of the primary goals of Sukyo Mahikari is to develop and elevate the inner aspect of our minds, also called our innermost attitude, to attune with divine wisdom. This allows the vibrations of pure love and harmony to increase and emanate through our minds, influencing our motives, perceptions, thoughts, words, and actions. Our mind's reflective capacity increases too, so we are better able to grasp the deep spiritual meaning in our daily life experiences. We naturally begin to perceive the unseen and the seen, or the spiritual and material, in our lives.

By the elevation of our reflective minds, our connection, perception, and realizations become connected with that which is greater than ourselves and to which we are truly and purposefully connected. Such development of our reflective mind allows us to begin seeing through our spiritual eye, which I like to call the window of the soul. We become aware of our true self (or soul) and spirit. This directly-felt connection allows us to also develop directly-seen connection that puts us on a deep inside-out course on which we can naturally cultivate our inherent virtues for the benefit of others. By "others" I mean to include our families and societies, so their happiness and our own may grow in harmony with God's will and a peaceful civilization may materialize, step by step, throughout the world.

In the past, such elevation of the reflective mind has been associated with sages and saints living outside society. But now we know that every person has an inner life, which, when cultivated through contemplative practice, offers us all an opportunity to raise our consciousness and elevate our innermost attitude. Giving and receiving True Light and practicing the universal principles of Sukyo Mahikari in daily life allows any human being within society to elevate the reflective mind to that of a saint or sage. Integrating spirituality in daily life—through commitment to pure and genuine practices—connects the pure vibration of the true self with the flow of divine wisdom and love. Such development naturally finds expression in altruistic actions reflecting each individual person's special virtues.

Thus the most significant, direct result of spiritual elevation is the transformation of our lives, our spirits, minds, and bodies so that we live in harmony, happiness, and true peace in society. As this vibration of peace contained in our relationship with God begins to permeate our relationships with ourselves, with others, and with nature, it spreads to the larger human family through connected relationships—one person, one family, one community, and one nation at a time.

At times we experience especially holy moments filled with divinefulness or spiritfulness, which can be defined as feeling full of the vibrations of divine energy and harmony and connection with others. One of the most memorable moments of my life took place at Sukyo Mahikari's 50th Anniversary Grand Ceremony at Suza, where I performed on the grand stage in a Broadway musical-style dance offered by the North American region. After much anticipation, the celebration began with the Australia-Oceana region performing an aboriginal dance, followed by a dance by the Latin American region which expressed traditionally distinct male and female roles. The Asian region danced an amalgam of classical and modern dance and the Europe-African region sang opera and danced the waltz. The North American region's performance in which I danced concluded the event with a theatrical frontier barn raising set to Aaron Copeland's "Rodeo." As I prepared to take the stage I had a profound spiritual experience. It was dark where I waited in the wings, peering out into the audience where I saw in the royal box above the stage the two holy masters, Seishusama and Oshienushisama, standing side by side. I felt an immediate heart connection with them and felt their deep and profoundly elevated harmony. I felt joy. I knew then that everything in the dance would be flawless and, indeed, every minute detail was. The performance was tremendous, but even more significant was the way we experienced the expression of the human capacity to elevate the mind to harmony with God. I felt this harmony in spirit fill my mind and body—perhaps even the whole human presence—with divinefulness and spiritfulness. I have felt this harmony and deep peace as well as a sense of order in the flow of activity for all on many other occasions, but the 50th Anniversary Grand Ceremony is one such experience I will never forget.

Circles

I have always approached my life relationally, so naturally, I wanted to bring this approach to my professional life. My first book is called *Circles in the Nursery: Practicing Multicultural Family Therapy* because my professional work and my spiritual work both happen to thrive in small, organically connected groups set up to work together deeply. Dan Siegel's work inspires me as I pursue a project I call Circles. The relational approach is grounded in the universal principle of standing in each other's shoes and acknowledging each other's help. In other words, we embrace the attitude that relationships and empathy in relationships is more important than individuality—thus learning to give of ourselves and take care of others, lessening self-centeredness and growing the joy of selfless pure love and harmony. The practice of giving Light and then reflecting with others in a circle fosters this awareness, helping people trust each other, cooperate, appreciate each other, and connect deeply in relationships.

For many years I had been offering clinical supervision to a team of psychotherapists I was contracted to supervise by the mental health division of a Southern California non-profit organization. I had been incorporating self-awareness development practices in this clinical supervision using a method and model I featured in my first book. In 2011, opportunities came to share spiritual practice and engage in deeper personal reflection exercises designed to tap into inner wisdom, divine spark, professional compassion, and empathy.

The CEO of the organization I served was a Stanford Business School alumnus with much experience running non-profit organizations, but the unique challenges of running a human services organization gave him reason to think outside the box. Founded in 1986 to meet the needs of the growing numbers of infants and young children suffering from trauma in Los Angeles, this organization at that time served more than 19,000 children, youth, and families in Southern California. The CEO was committed to the preparation and development of his staff of clinicians to meet the needs of this most vulnerable population. I had introduced him to the director (who we call Dojocho) of the Pasadena Sukyo Mahikari Center at the time. After receiving Light a few times, the CEO invited Dojocho and me to speak to three hundred employees at his organization's all staff retreat. About thirty-five people received Light after the retreat, and I was invited to create a program designed to help the staff develop a greater capacity for reflection.

The program was led by a team of colleagues from psychology and Sukyo Mahikari. If people wanted to receive Light, they could go to the Pasadena Center separately. Thus the Circles pilot ran for six months, training three groups: the CEO's executive team, the organization's mental health team in Pasadena, and the most experienced psychotherapists in the organization across offices. Each group met for three hours once a month. The participants reported that the executive team was strengthened by the program (the CEO called them his "dream team"), and many of the participants described their work environment as warmer and more productive than before. It was a rich experience.

Since then, the Circles team has been self-training to grow together spiritually and create a program of Light and reflection for leaders. At present, the Circles team leaders spread over different cities go to the Sukyo Mahikari center nearest them to give and receive Light and meet every month via Zoom video conference to develop and practice twenty spirit-centered exercises designed to strengthen the reflective mind and develop its capacities for directly-felt connection and directly-seen connection.

The Circles experience is grounded in the universal principle or law of spirit-mind-body that governs everything in the spiritual and physical realms of the universe. The spirit has the primary influence, followed by the mind, and then the body. Within the human being our true self/soul/spirit emanates vibrations that influence our minds and actions. When our vibrations, thoughts, and actions are motivated by selflessness and love for others we are spirit-centered, and when they are focused on oneself, attached to money, relationships, and other things, we are material-centered. Giving True Light is the most direct way to cut through from the conscious, to the subconscious, to the deepest consciousness and vibration of the true self. It leaves people energized, takes away the static of the mind, and light bulbs go off—giving people realizations and insight-strengthening intuition.

The Circles program format is quite simple, but the content runs deep. We invite people to give and receive Light first for fifty minutes and then reflect together, usually for at least two hours, using one of the spirit-centeredness exercises. This helps each participant to develop spirit-centeredness and fullness of spirit in the mind and body. Each Circles meeting concludes with a quick evaluation that we use to gather data on how well the process is going. It's truly an experience of both spiritfulness and divinefulness.

The series of twenty Circles reflection exercises focuses on helping participants elevate their innermost attitude and develop personal and collective virtues. Thus a Circles group can meet once to taste divinefulness, to give and receive Light, and practice one spirit-centered exercise that fits well for the group at that point in time. Or it can meet successively to dive into divinefulness to give and receive Light each time and practice several or all the spirit-centered exercises one by one. The first ten exercises relate to elevating vibrations of gratitude, acceptance, humility, and harmony. The next ten exercises include self-narrative to elevate vibration of true purpose, pure love, communication, intuition, and discernment. After giving Light to the Circles group participants, Circles leaders demonstrate each exercise following this simple structure: they choose a story that relates to the theme of the exercise evoking gratitude, joy, or happiness and reflecting on its meaning using a series of reflection questions. This is followed by group reflection and feedback, dialogue, and integration of learning from deep inside-out. After the leaders' demonstration, Circles group participants take their turn to follow suit, one by one sharing their stories and reflection questions, receiving the group engagement and support in the same way.

Thus, in Circles, members of the group support each other in reflecting and learning from deep within—integrating personal insights, realizations, and wisdom that they hold preciously together. This experience complements and integrates the mind's outside-in day-to-day learning of facts and information that takes place through living in society. As the integrated mind receives the Light of God, it has the chance to begin purifying, attuning, and elevating at the depth of innermost attitude to the will of God. This gradually opens the way for scientists and all people to discern divine wisdom. The Circles program of directly experiencing Light giving and practicing reflection through spirit-centeredness exercises is intended to cultivate universal principles through the elevation of mind. These principles include the diligent practice of Light giving, spreading the Light and principles, expressing gratitude concretely, following the will of God in an accepting way, practicing genuine humility, making concessions and acknowledging the help of others, maintaining purity of the body, soul, and physical environment, maintaining cleanliness and tidiness, avoiding waste and using materials efficiently, and maintaining a calm mind acting in a smiling, orderly manner.

It's not difficult to imagine how and why these virtues would be helpful for people working in the field of clinical psychology, but really, doesn't every field benefit from such personal development? The combination of Light and reflection helps people of every profession, every creed, every socio-economic background, every age, gender, and ethnicity elevate the mind to a consciousness that is more spirit-centered and less encumbered by the material pitfalls of our day. By gathering regularly for three-hour retreat sessions to help one another see through the mind's eye, which Dan Siegel describes as "the capacity for the human mind to see itself," and by elevating this capacity for self-awareness, participants gradually begin seeing through spiritual eyes. This is the mind seeing the mind itself and the world through the torchlight of the soul. Harmonizing with God's Light and universal principles creates felt harmony, both deep and true, to build community and trust. This is the hope of Circles: to give people such a way to grow together and to scientifically capture this human development and its natural, positive impact on human-nature harmony, which also impacts the preservation of nature.

Giving and receiving Light, reflection, connection, integration, and consolidation are all built into the Circles group format. We also discuss some difficult topics like taming the ego, transforming fear and negativity to love and compassion, realizing equality in difference, and addressing childhood memories—although we focus on positive experiences or those that no longer evoke pain. We are not a psychotherapy group, but rather a group focused on harmonizing with the divine and elevating the spiritual vibration and reflective capacity of our minds through deep, positive experiences and connected relationships. Thus we even find ourselves expressing gratitude for any negative emotions as we forge onward into lives of service focused on the betterment of our human family.

God's Will in Disguise

Sometimes we have friends join us at Circles self-training meetings. On one such occasion in January 2019, Roger Beck joined Circles as we practiced an exercise on acceptance of the will of God. At approximately the mid-point of the two-hour training session, participants were asked to think of an experience where we had been unable to forgive someone. Roger recounted the story of how in his role as a university professor he had not forgiven his dean of faculty for something he had said decades ago during a departmental meeting where they were considering whether a young faculty member should be granted tenure. The dean was not interested in whether the person in question had met the criteria for being granted tenure. Rather, the key question from the dean's point of view was whether they could hire someone better if they denied this person tenure. Roger was outraged at the dean's willingness to ignore the university's written rules and procedures for granting tenure. If this young faculty member had met the criteria for tenure, denying him that status would damage him personally—not to mention compromising the integrity of the university. Decades later, Roger didn't know how to forgive the dean. The Circles facilitator explained that forgiveness was a tool for practicing acceptance and offered the following exercise: for several minutes, the group prayed: "I forgive [the person's name]" while focused on feelings of compassion and love, closing with the prayer "I accept [the person named]."

After doing this exercise, Roger was happy to report improvement in his feelings toward the dean—but he still couldn't really say he had successfully forgiven him. Then the facilitator pointed out that the dean's role had been that of purification, that is, to cleanse Roger by removing some of Roger's spiritual impurities. Suddenly Roger's mind grasped the truth in that statement, and his forgiveness was complete. Roger recounted an example from the primary spiritual development course this experience brought to mind: when you're standing in the train and someone steps on your foot, be grateful to them! Your impurities are being eliminated. Roger was relieved and very grateful to have given up this long-standing resentment, and to have learned a useful process for dealing with any other resentments he might develop in the future. He can simply use the forgiveness exercise from this training, remembering that whatever makes us angry and resentful is a cleansing lovingly designed by God to eliminate some of our impurities.

Writer Paula D'Arcy famously said, "God comes to you disguised as your life." Whether God appears as a painful series of purifications or in the comforting beauty of a sunrise, we can pay attention with focus and humility. Roger shared with me another story that very much fits this pattern of humble awareness when I asked him how he decided to become a college professor. He confessed that he really had not planned to earn a PhD in economics or become a professor. In his formative years, his goal had been to accumulate personal wealth in the business world. After completing a Master's degree in Business Administration (MBA), he worked five years in public accounting and management consulting. In that fifth year, he was shaken to the core when his employer told him he did not have the ability to be a management consultant and promptly fired him.

I'm sure Roger isn't the only person for whom a career crisis left them in this conundrum of what to do next, but he was deeply devastated. Roger was twenty-seven years old, newly married, and his life's plan had been dealt a fatal blow. His BS from MIT, MBA from Northwestern, and the CPA he had earned through passing a two-and-a-half day comprehensive examination felt like nothing more than alphabet soup tacked onto his name at this point in his life. Herein lies the gift: of course at the time all he felt was bad, but with hindsight, he can see that this was the best thing that could have happened to him because it forced him to take a new reading on life from his inner compass. Was he still committed to the personal mission of accumulating as much personal wealth as possible? A better question he asked himself was "Who am I, really? How do I relate to other people? What should my role and purpose in society be?" This is precisely the type of inner reflective capacity we cultivate in Circles. Roger's former boss inadvertently gave him the gift of reflection by firing him at the tender age of twenty-seven.

It's odd for me to think of Roger as someone who might have devoted his life to money rather than to God and the betterment of society. Thankfully, he decided to abandon his original plan, which he now sees was based in a combination of fear of the unknown and hedonism. Just as the United States Marine Corps had harshly re-shaped Roger's previously non-athletic physical body through the strenuous physical routine of boot camp, Roger's worldview was reshaped by the harsh realities of the dog-eat-dog world of finance. His inner compass told him to find a way to make a contribution to society while earning sufficient financial resources to adequately support his family. This might not seem like such a big shift, but for Roger it was this decision that caused his life to become aligned with the universal principle to work for the benefit of others and society, making him the person I know today. I'm not sure I would recognize the person Roger might have become had God not intervened in this abrupt career change.

Roger's view of economics had already begun to shift during his years in public accounting and management consulting. Even as he worked as an auditor and management consultant, Roger enjoyed reading about and discussing political economy, more as a hobby than as a profession. Having read Ayn Rand's *Atlas Shrugged* as an undergraduate, he explored Objectivism and other economic theories that held much more meaning to him than the pure economics he had learned in the classroom at MIT, which had no obvious connection to life and society.

After he was fired from his job, his goal was to find a university where he could study economics as a meaningful discipline, not as a set of abstractions separated from reality. He chose to pursue his doctoral work at University of Chicago because their economics department had a distinct reputation for taking a more applied approach to academic study with an emphasis on free markets, which at the time, was Roger's interest. He was happy to work with many prominent faculty members whose normative economic views aligned with Roger's then-held belief in the ideal of competitive private markets populated by profit-maximizing businesses with little government intervention. Roger was spellbound by Adam Smith's concept of the invisible hand: businesses seeking to maximize profits in a competitive market would cause the market as a whole to yield socially desirable outcomes—as if guided by an invisible hand. Looking back, he can see how this may have been an awakening moment for Roger as he began to recognize unseen powers, even if they were economic markets.

Of course now he sees things differently, but Roger was very happy with his learning experience at Chicago. Even though many of his peers pursued abstract economic topics, he was allowed to write a dissertation based on three case studies of landmark antitrust cases involving patents. With much of his data coming from Supreme Court briefs, he derived numbers from the texts, patent data, and contracts found in these records. Thus, the University of Chicago nourished Roger's hunger for the kind of reality-based economics which had attracted him to the field in the first place. This would all come to be very meaningful indeed, as Roger gave up the pursuit of money as his raison d'être, he began to recognize economics as both extremely important and very interesting and, from then on, dedicated his working life to teaching.

With the much more pure and lofty goal of helping students master the fundamentals of economics, and as a result become better citizens, choose more wisely between competing political agendas/parties/candidates, and make better personal economic decisions, Roger became an associate professor in the School of Business at the University of Alberta. He was deeply committed to his students, both undergrads and MBA students. Improving his students' learning was his first priority. To that end, he issued end-of-term surveys inviting them to show him how to better help them learn. Looking back, Roger tells me this process taught him the importance of humility. By humbly accepting his students' criticism, Roger was able to become a better teacher. He learned new teaching practices in various workshops, while helping other professors improve by volunteering to consult with them as one of the university's "peer consultants."

Having developed newfound humility through teaching, Roger developed relationships with his students that energized him. In his words, "Helping my students left me with a warm glow." He began to respect his students in a way that is consistent with the universal principle that every person has a spark of divinity within them. Roger was sure he had made the right decision in becoming an economics professor, and his efforts were recognized in a number of prestigious awards. Just as important to him was the way his students were generally enthusiastic about his courses and felt they learned a great deal by taking them. His students appreciated his efforts and seemed to like him personally.

As one of ten 3M Fellows selected to participate in a three-day seminar on teaching and learning, Roger was taught that the pedagogical method of devoting class time exclusively to lecture was no longer considered a best practice. Lecturing was less effective in promoting student learning than alternative methods aimed at encouraging students to become more responsible for mastering the material on their own time. Although Roger agreed with this shift away from lecture-based learning, he felt he was too busy with research and other responsibilities to commit the time it would take to rework his courses. Consequently, between 1986 and 1992, he only made a few small changes to achieve minor reductions in the amount of class time spent lecturing.

1986 was also the year Roger took the primary spiritual development course and began to follow Sukyo Mahikari spiritual practices. Thus began a gradual process in which his spiritual practices changed him, thereby changing his academic life in fundamental and important ways. Giving and receiving True Light was at the core of these spiritual practices. In accordance with the universal principle of spirit first, followed by mind, then body, Roger recognized that his soul and spiritual body were being purified when he received and gave True Light. Similarly, his mind and physical body were also being purified. Removal of impurities at these three levels naturally changes a person. Roger noticed that his relations with his academic colleagues—as well as with his family members—became more harmonious. His level of stress fell and his rheumatoid arthritis completely disappeared.

He continued to re-attend primary spiritual development courses. Gradually, as God eliminated more and more impurities, Roger's understanding of the universal principles deepened. Step by step, he moved toward making receiving True Light a daily practice. For decades now, he has seldom missed a day. He's deeply grateful to God for allowing him to have the arrangements needed in his life to consistently receive True Light each day. In hindsight, he can see how much of his history has been re-written from disappointment and hardship to gratitude for every purification.

Roger embraced the three great virtues—gratitude, humility, and acceptance—and by practicing these virtues and training in them, he began to improve his innermost attitude. To the extent we practice gratitude, we will be happier. Humility smoothes our interactions with others, reduces conflict in our life, and fosters greater acceptance, thus reducing frustration and stress while contributing to happiness. Following the Sukyo Mahikari spiritual path brings opportunities to elevate spiritually in a variety of ways. Giving and receiving True Light elevates us by eliminating impurities sometimes referred to as negative karma, but studying and applying universal principles like gratitude, humility, and acceptance in daily life also leads to spiritual elevation. There are additional ways to progress spiritually, such as attending spiritual events like monthly thanksgiving ceremonies at a Sukyo Mahikari center or traveling to grand ceremonies in Japan, re-attending primary spiritual development courses, and attending higher-level spiritual development courses. Making efforts to be of service to God and others in a variety of ways also reduces our impurities.

As we eliminate impurities and elevate spiritually, we are better able to change our actions in ways that harmonize with the Divine will. Changes in us help to create a civilization that will place the spiritual dimension first and the material dimension second. Obviously, our present modern civilization is dominated by materialistic goals and thinking. Thus, we have a huge shift ahead of us to achieve a spirit-first civilization. Sukyo Mahikari, and all the other organizations in the world that cultivate and encourage spirit-first thought and action, have much work to do. Roger credits the Sukyo Mahikari spiritual practices he followed with changing his life. As it turns out, he would face another professional crisis before his career was complete, through which God continued to purify his soul.

Putting the Teacher to the Test

It was Roger's usual practice about two weeks after a course began to randomly select two students to serve as a feedback committee. One day, he would turn the class over to the feedback committee fifteen minutes before the end of class and then leave the room. The committee would ask their classmates two questions: first, what things are helping your learning in this course, and second, what might be changed to further enhance your learning? After class, the feedback committee would go to Roger's office and discuss their classmates' answers to these two questions with him. Over the years, Roger had grown used to the positive and warmly supportive comments collected by each feedback committee. There was almost no criticism, although sometimes he was asked to make minor changes to tweak improvements in student learning. Imagine Roger's shock and consternation when he heard harsh criticism from the feedback committee in his MBA Managerial Economics course in the fall of 1992. Nothing was going well. Students were not learning, despite spending far more time on his course than other courses. They were extremely unhappy and angry with Roger. The suddenness of this change was like night and day, and, in one sense, hard to explain, because nothing major had changed since the course was last delivered earning hearty accolades from students. But in retrospect, once again, we can see how God had prepared Roger to take a major leap forward in his academic career in order to greatly enhance students' learning. One of these needed changes was finding how to make students more engaged in their own learning—the major insight from the 1986 3M Fellows' seminar that he had not yet fully implemented.

Roger had a full-blown professional crisis on his hands. Had he achieved sufficient change through his efforts to elevate spiritually to successfully meet this challenge? Like so many of us, Roger could not see this question at the time, nor was his conscious mind bringing universal principles to bear. But he did realize that he was in the midst of a major cleansing phenomenon. In the primary spiritual development course, he had learned that—in addition to eliminating impurities through all the active methods described above—God also arranges for us to eliminate impurities through what is known as passive compensation. There are many kinds of passive compensation including illness, financial loss, disaster, and emotional pain. There is generally and steadily less passive compensation for those who choose to actively eliminate impurities with commitment and diligence, but passive compensation cannot be entirely avoided.

It's important to receive passive compensation with both gratitude and apology. Roger needed to be grateful for this emotionally trying experience for two reasons. First, this painful compensation was an opportunity to eliminate some negative karma. Second, if he chose not to meet this crisis with gratitude, but instead with resistance, anger, and dissatisfaction, the negative spiritual vibrations from these emotions would create toxins in his body—which would add to his spiritual impurities—potentially obliterating any spiritual gains from this cleansing and preventing him from tuning in to God's will. So he knew he needed to express apology and humbly offer prayers to God, expressing both gratitude and apology. Roger—who once dreamed of acquiring great wealth— also made a special monetary offering to materialize his gratitude. And then he materialized his gratitude and apology by developing a process to transform a learning disaster into an enhanced learning experience. As a former professor myself, I very much relate to his story. But what's most interesting to anyone of any profession, is how Roger's professional crisis became his personal transformation. The next part of the story reveals Roger's deep, inner change of heart.

Success in the academic life is often measured and driven by ego. Professors tend to believe they are right even when students point out their clear mistakes. In fact, one of Roger's respected colleagues recommended that he ignore his students' protests, assuming the problem was unfounded and would disappear eventually. But remembering the universal principles of gratitude, humility, and acceptance, Roger saw a need and an opportunity to practice all three. Students paraded to his office one after the other to protest assigned grades, revealing a high level of student dissatisfaction and unrest. As Roger reflected on how he had been dealing with these complaints, he realized that he had done so in a very rational and emotionless fashion, coolly explaining why the assigned grade was the correct grade and taking no account of the emotions of the complainer—the disappointment, anger, and shame for these unexpected low grades. As a general rule, Roger had been pretty nearly devoid of empathy. But because of his spiritual practices, his mind's reflective capacity had been enlarged. He could finally clearly see the need to have—and to express—empathy for the emotions students were feeling.

At the beginning of the next class, Roger considered explicitly apologizing for his unfeeling behavior. But then he decided it might be sufficient to just ignore the past and simply adopt a more empathic approach when interacting with students in the future. Just at that moment, an irate student in the third row pointed his thermos at him like a rifle. Roger took the hint and decided he needed to publicly acknowledge his fault. (God is always generous with humility training right when we need it most!) Roger seized that moment to sincerely apologize to his class for his unfeeling methods of dealing with their grading complaints and promised to make amends. The class broke into spontaneous applause and broad smiles. Roger smiled just as broadly as he told me about this experience almost thirty years later. He genuinely felt good about having humbly realized his fault, apologizing, and having his apology accepted by the class.

Having spent decades in academia, I can attest to the rarity of a professor showing such vulnerability and humility to anyone, much less to their students. Placing priority on teaching as a way to serve society in a genuine and humble way is quite extraordinary in university cultures that tend to reward grant-funded research over teaching. As a professor of economics, Roger was clearly being transformed by his spiritual practices to the degree that he could see God appearing to him disguised as his life.

Even as he shared this story with me with the added wisdom of hindsight, Roger admits he is still learning from this experience, recognizing it as a major cleansing that arrived as a seemingly disastrous career low point, but with an adjustment in attitude shaped by spiritual principles of humility and empathy, ended up being one of the most important points of Roger's academic career—

just as he now sees his rheumatoid arthritis as one of the most important points of his life because it led him to grow spiritually.

As a result of this student revolt, Roger made significant changes to his teaching methodology, communication style, and pedagogy. He went on to publish articles about this experience, presenting the pedagogical changes he made at academic conferences so other professors might bring some of these methods to their own classrooms. His original purpose in becoming a teacher came to fruition when he realized that his profession was meant to be built upon pure altruism. Although in 1992 Roger's overall rating as an instructor was the lowest he had received in twenty years of teaching, his overall rating returned to elevated levels with use of the new system in 1993. In 1995 and 1996, he won the business school award for excellence in teaching in the MBA program. Roger attests that he could not have met the challenges presented to him in the fall of 1992 without having carried out the Sukyo Mahikari spiritual practices that enabled him to grow spiritually, thus developing the abilities needed to find a new teaching methodology more consistent with universal principles. Quite likely, without the necessary spiritual growth, God may not have arranged this crisis to challenge him, and Roger would not have become a fit instrument for constructive change.

Roger shifted from a teaching system that encouraged competition between students to one that fostered cooperation. His previous method of "grading on the curve" penalizes cooperation because choosing to help other students in cooperative study sessions could move them up the grade distribution to the disadvantage of the person who helped them. Roger's new course design assigned grades according to levels of learning with no artificial limitation on the number of A's and B's he assigned. The new design replaced selfish competition with cooperation and rewarded efforts to help others learn, which made a huge difference spiritually. The new system also required students to take greater responsibility for their own learning by completing reading and research assignments rather than passively listening to the lectures. The result of a more spiritually elevated pedagogy was a huge increase in students' learning and the creation of a more compassionate and collaborative environment. And so, Roger's pedagogical evolution followed his spiritual evolution, both as a result of and contributing to the elevation of the mind.

Elevated Economics

This change followed Roger beyond the classroom when he retired from full-time teaching in 1997. Having participated in Sukyo Mahikari spiritual practices for over a decade, Roger saw the academic discipline of economics very differently at the end of his career than he did early in his career. Not only was his teaching approach redirected by his spiritual transformation, his perspective on his academic field was completely overhauled. He could see clearly that the dominant effect of most 20th-century economic models supported the material-first character of our society. In retrospect, it really isn't surprising that endorsement of profit maximization as the engine of social well-being promotes materialism. Roger attributes his ability to see this flaw in the economic model to the opening of his spiritual eyes.

Roger now sees profit maximization in a complex way in terms of universal principles, one aspect of which is minimization of total costs. In order to maximize profits, businesses must minimize costs. This is consistent with the universal principle to treat materials preciously, avoiding waste. God has placed all the things we use to produce products and services within our reach. Showing our gratitude to God for these precious resources, so essential to our physical well-being, means we should not waste them. Another aspect of profit maximization, according to Roger, is that it fails to ensure there will be no detrimental effects from each business's operation on people and society. The profit maximization principle is neutral toward negative effects.

Typically, negative effects are seen as "externalities," meaning they are external to a business's calculation of revenues and costs. Businesses usually ignore externalities when they maximize profits. Profit maximization does not require businesses to have a net positive effect. Thus, profit maximization does not rule out polluting the environment, damaging the health of customers by manufacturing things like cigarettes and pharmaceuticals with serious side effects, processed foods, etc., evading and even violating regulatory restrictions as long as fines are less than the profits gained through illegal activities, and making political contributions to purchase favorable government programs and policies that transfer resources from citizens to business owners. Roger now argues that failure to offset negative effects with appropriate compensation—or to prevent negative effects in the first place—is a major flaw in our economic system. Permitted activities clash with the universal principle to be altruistic, not selfish, in our treatment of others and to care for the environment preciously. An altruistic outcome would find customers and citizens either better off, or at worst no worse off, from the operations of a business.

The research Roger has done and the experiences he's had since retiring from teaching have made him keenly aware—for the first time—of how poorly our economic system performs when assessed against the standard of the well-being of our society and its citizens. While recognizing that there are some conscious, elevated businesses that refuse to operate in a way that would harm their customers or other citizens, Roger notes that they deliberately focus on service to their customers and care of the environment in addition to maximizing profits. His perception that such businesses are relatively uncommon exceptions to deliberate profit maximization, regardless of its effects on customers or other citizens, reveals that the principles of economics we are teaching today are not consistent with universal principles, including altruistic love for others, care for the environment, and adherence to the spirit/mind/body principle. Instead, Roger points out that our economic principles hold material gains to be the primary and ultimate goal, as well as the most important criterion for assessing our economy's success.

As you can see, Roger's approach to the discipline of economics was turned 180 degrees by the elevation of his mind.

With Spirit First, All Else Follows

I'm so grateful to know Roger's story of transformation as a teacher, as an economist, and as a human being. Giving and receiving True Light, engaging the spirit-mind-body principle, deepening my mind's reflective capacity, and applying universal principles in daily life has changed my approach to teaching as well. Engaging with the depths of my soul has become a form of life-long internal education for me. These developments within myself inspire me to find ways to encourage students at all levels as I learn alongside them how to better integrate spirituality in our lives, thus engaging with the depths of the true self. Including this goal among the purposes of education would re-vitalize the field of education, make it life advancing, and nudge us toward a more peaceful civilization.

Roger hopes that by giving precedence to spirit, followed by attention to the secondary and tertiary mental and physical dimensions, we might shift the path of education to prioritizing learning from deep inside-out (including personal spiritual development), making it complementary to the currently dominant outside-in learning. I must agree with Roger in his assertion that humanity would achieve higher educational goals more effectively by including human spiritual development as a foundational element of education. By being in harmony with divine will, education would prepare people to be in harmony with their true selves, with nature, and with each other.

Roger Beck's story is important on many levels. His professional life illustrates the conscious shift he made personally from self-centered motivation to selfless motivation. He continues to engage in elevating and deepening his mind's spirit-centeredness and reflective capacity. This is why he joins the Circles leaders self training group to train himself to continue to elevate his innermost attitude as it manifests in interpersonal communications and diversity. The change he made from competitively organized learning to collaboratively engaged learning was accomplished through a deep inner shift. His spiritual practice opened him up to reflection and humble effort to improve himself for the sake of others. The change was not at the level of ideas alone. He changed as a person from deep inside-out in the vibration of his innermost attitude, motivation, and commitment to spirit-centeredness. And as he grows, he develops more wisdom as a human being.

The model of spirit-mind-body education, or deep inside-out education, provides us with an enormous opportunity. As educators commit to growing spiritually and living spirit-first lives, students will naturally gravitate toward learning and working together in teams and groups, collaborating, growing kinder, more connected, more responsible, and more responsive to the invitation to contribute their part toward the long-term betterment of the world and the generations to come. This is the foundation of true confidence and true happiness.

Elevating the Mind in the Family Pod

My husband David's opportunity to grow spiritually came late in life when he received his holy omitama. When I first met him he was already in his middle years. He had trained in applied physics at the University of Pennsylvania and was blessed to have meaningful work in engineering throughout his career. But his true love was astronomy. As a boy of thirteen he bought a telescope with his lawn mowing earnings to teach himself his way around the sky. Yet as a young man he thought there may not be enough jobs for astronomers, so he chose to become an engineer. He was not centered in spirit deeply enough to know that when we commit to our true purpose there is always a way to go forward in the world and contribute to that purpose.

In mid-life the opportunity to come closer to astronomy came again when he moved from the Plasma Physics lab at Princeton University to Caltech's Jet Propulsion Laboratory to work on calibrating the wide field and planetary camera-2 on the Hubble Space Telescope. At this time, my four-year-old son Rudy and I moved in next door to David in Pasadena, California. I saw his attunement with the divine through the laws of physics when he explained his work to me. I did not express this in spiritual terms at the time, though, not yet having a spiritual practice of my own to help me do so. I could also see from early on that he was pursuing a path that was allied to his true purpose, though not centered in it. Ten years after we were married, I received my holy omitama and began to nurture him spiritually by giving him Light and inviting him to come to Sukyo Mahikari centers with me. Eight years later, in February 2010, he received his holy omitama.

Almost immediately, he experienced great pressure at work and came to the conclusion that the input of a particular scientist on the other side of the country was needed in very short order to solve the problem. But David did not have a way to access this person. Unsure of how to proceed without that specific expert's input, he went over to a colleague's office to report his realization. Before he could say a word, a stranger entered the room and was introduced as the person David needed to hear from. This person gave all the needed input to beautifully resolve all matters in hand. David had spent his life with the mindset that science and religion belong in different boxes, with science being his primary devotion. David believed in God but was yet to do much more to honor this awareness, assuming God was not particularly engaged in the affairs of the world. Synchronicities like the very person he needed to see walking in the room as he was about to express this need belie other possibilities, but David remained a skeptic nonetheless.

And so, it was wonderful to receive these handwritten words from him in 2017 on our 25th wedding anniversary, seven years after he began giving Light:

> "You have brought a hard-nosed realist, some would say pessimist, to Su God. Years ago, I would have said I believe in God, but would not have dwelt on the subject long. Not so now. I do struggle with various matters, but that means engagement. Something new for me. Please understand that that itself is a long way for me to have come. Thank you."

One of the changes I have observed in him since he began giving Light is that the continuous underlying anxiety he once had about stability in his work has eased up. He is more confident now, in addition to being passionate and diligent, which he has always been. Twelve years ago, when it was time for me to make a switch from contributing in the world through professional channels to concentrating on divine service and spiritual development, David surprised me by being able to fully support this spirit-centered step for me to concentrate on spiritual development with our family, friends, and spiritual community. He embraced my awareness that it was time for me to be the change I hoped to see in the world. It was a moment of seeing through his spiritual eyes and elevating the material-centered striving of his young adulthood to spirit-centeredness. I was amazed and grateful. This moment of amazement will remain in my spiritual eye as all spiritual experiences remain indelible in the minds of people.

Another change I've witnessed in David is the ultimate purpose of the work he has the opportunity to do now. He has been given the opportunity to study the nature of small meteors that approach the earth with the long-term vision of possibly detecting larger ones in future, exploring ways to gently deflect their trajectories. The ultimate purpose, then, of safeguarding the earth and humanity, connected with the principle to treat creation preciously, is a new potential purpose in David's work (which has thus far been focused on discovery and instrumentation for discovery.) It is inspiring to see how his compassion for others has grown and silently integrated into his work. I asked him if Light giving could help his peers attain their goals. He said he imagined it would, through personal development and increasing harmony. As science and spirituality reunite as the unified fields they have truly always been, I imagine we will see great strides in scientific discoveries focused on the betterment of life for the earth and all its inhabitants, as well as the vast cosmos that captured David's imagination as a child.

David received his holy omitama at the Pasadena Center one month after my father passed away in Noida, outside New Delhi, India. This most deeply painful loss for me and for our whole larger family was a divine arrangement for the elevation of both souls—my father's to the astral world and David's toward divine service in the physical world—something I could perceive despite my profound grief. This realization helped me to offer gratitude for both arrangements and destinies. My prayer for David now is that in his eternal journey he be blessed to offer service to God and astronomy. For this will be a path of joy for him.

The same year David received his holy omitama, the New Delhi Center was inaugurated in India. In the previous year I had gone twice to India to my ailing father's bedside. On the first visit in April I had taken our daughter Mira, almost thirteen at the time, with me. On the way we had a stopover for a few hours in Chicago. Out of nowhere I had the most intense pain come on, so much so that I was beginning to feel very weak and disoriented. To make matters worse, as I was about to board an international flight, I found myself needing repeated access to the restroom. I was at a loss as to what to do when I decided to speak with an airline employee who was getting ready to prepare the flight for boarding. I told her my plight. She walked up to me, took my hand, and said "Come with me, I will re-seat you near the restroom and board you right now. You can go to the restroom whenever you need to." Mira and I followed her. Once seated, I asked Mira to give me Light, which she began to radiate to the back of my kidneys. Within five minutes or so I felt strong, comfortable, and completely well. My cleansing was over. Mira and I were so grateful. At the same time, we noticed something had changed outside. It had begun snowing! Huge, soft snowflakes bigger than any I had ever seen, and the first Mira had ever seen, were falling softly from the sky. Mira was wonderstruck as she looked out of the airplane window. The plane, fully packed and boarded, was grounded for another three hours as it snowed. The pilot announced that we were experiencing an unseasonal Easter snowfall, which gave me the opportunity to give Light the whole time with gratitude.

On that trip, we met Light givers in New Delhi for the first time and they began coming to give Light to my family. We began going to the temporary New Delhi Center. The pain I had experienced at the airport provided a necessary cleansing in preparation for these spiritually important connections made in New Delhi for India and my family. Light givers had been earnestly preparing for a permanent center in New Delhi for three decades. New Delhi (being the capital of India) is the spiritual upstream of India.

On my next trip to New Delhi in the fall of that same year, I attended the groundbreaking ceremony for the new Sukyo Mahikari center. At the invitation of New Delhi Center members, I offered one of the prayers, standing with them by the side of a great hole in the ground where the center now stands. Though I was inclined to remain at my father's bedside, I remember well how he encouraged me to go and participate, with his face bright and shining up at me. About eleven months later, this center held its first primary spiritual development course and my youngest sister Shouma received her holy omitama. Now, ten years later, as we are unable to travel freely during the

COVID-19 pandemic, it gives me joy to know that Shouma is becoming more active in her Light giving and is giving Light to our mother regularly.

In these final months of the tumultuous year 2020, I keenly realize that elevation of the mind and the innermost attitude is crucial, as it manifests and reflects in the elevation of the spiritual condition of the physical world as well, bringing with it elevated ways of living and working. My immediate family unit is fortunate to be going through this extraordinary time of pandemic offering service to God while living together in our family pod. We do our best to give and receive Light daily, and though our Sukyo Mahikari centers are closed, we have welcomed the opportunity to care for the holy objects kept there. This divine service is a blessing for us to continue to deepen our spirit-centeredness and elevate our minds. We are grateful to be healthy, to find joy in work and study from home, care for others, physical exercise, and daily care for each other and our garden. We are also immensely blessed to unite with our center and family to embark on the design and construction of a small building to establish a small Sukyo Mahikari home center on our property in Pasadena. Our architect son Ives has been blessed to design the building and has submitted its plans to the city for a permit. When the building is ready, we look forward to welcoming holy Goshintai, the holy scroll through which people can harmonize themselves with God. My prayer is for one of my children to be my helper, with all my children and family united as one to welcome holy Goshintai. It is our effort as a family, united with all Light givers, to elevate the radiance of divine energy in this area and the world, conduct Circles in this sacred space, and use it to nurture spiritually-related souls to elevate their minds, families, and fields.

Chapter 2

Spotlights

Shamini Jain, PhD

What is the role of Spirit in inquiry, and therefore in science and education? In this chapter we learn from the wise experience of Dr. Leena Banerjee Brown as she shares her and others' journeys as they discover that the true power of the mind is informed not by our materially-based conditioning or by academic degrees, but by the unconditional love of Spirit. Leena describes how the spiritual practice of giving Light, alongside reflective relational circles, can elevate both our individual and collective minds—not only to bring us sanity in a chaotic society, but also to create thriving right relationships for the world, which we know are possible. If you want to be inspired by the power of spiritual practice to transform ways of learning and help solve humanity's biggest challenges, read this book.

Karen Eastman, PhD

There are many spaces and communities, including academic institutions, where the mind is valued above, and sometimes to the denial of, the spirit. Leena Banerjee Brown's stories of academics (herself included) reveal the possibilities of transformation when one lives a spirit-centered life and the spirit, mind, and body are in harmony. These personal experiences and observations serve as powerful inspiration for spiritual exploration and commitment to practices and the spiritual path.

Liza Auciello, PsyD

With all of the chaos, conflict, and division in our 2020 world, Leena's book is timely. To get to a place where peace, compassion, and acceptance reign, we need to give the Divine more space in our lives. Many people will "say a prayer" or "send light and blessings" to those who suffer but do little more to nurture their connection with the Divine. It is difficult to be psychologically healthy without a personal relationship with God. When we are able to tap into that pure place in our hearts, our "spiritual eye", our thoughts and reactions shift. We see things more clearly. What troubled us no longer has the same power. We forgive more easily. Our love for other beings and life itself intensifies. Leena describes the shift beautifully and is boldly bringing Light into the science of psychology and the world.

Chapter 3

Generation of Light

Sixteen-year-old Greta Thunberg was recognized as Time magazine's 2019 Person of the Year for mobilizing a worldwide effort to address climate change—the youngest person to receive this honor in the ninety-seven years the magazine has held this tradition. Indeed, it is the next generation that is modeling transformation on a global scale. While Greta Thunberg may be an extreme example of the power one young person can exert when she is grounded in principle, she is simultaneously emblematic of the type of global consciousness that characterizes the upcoming generations. Even before the COVID-19 pandemic sent a clear message that all inhabitants of the earth are interconnected, the children of the Digital Age (people born after 1980) were made aware of this reality through technology—which was a first language of sorts for many of them.

I would attest that spiritual awareness is actually all of humanity's first language, a common tongue that we all know at birth but eventually forget if it's not practiced in our family of origin and early childhood communities. And then, for many of us, later in life we find ourselves rediscovering, relearning, and reclaiming the fruits of spirituality through our commitment to spiritual practice. My story is no different. I treasure the deep awareness of the divine I had as a child in India, the warmth of my large extended family and close-knit community, and travel throughout the country. I felt a deep sense of belonging, groundedness, and freedom in our ancestral home in Kolkata, and in the other homes throughout India where we lived when I was a child—as well as in the magical Bengali summers spent in Santiniketan. Much spiritual nurturance took place in Santiniketan on the shores of the Kopai River, whether we were following along with sisters, cousins, and friends like little ducklings in a row behind my inspiring maternal grandfather or gathering around the dining table of my maternal grandmother's overflowing generosity. But it was in raising my own family that I reached for that wisdom and learning within. Later in life, I began to rekindle that divine spark and cultivate even greater transformation through the practices of giving and receiving True Light and engaging in the teachings of Sukyo Mahikari. How much more beneficial to the world would we all be if we could embrace continuously from early childhood the spiritual gifts that are every person's birthright?

The Spiritual Role of the Family Unit

Spiritual nurturance of the family and its next generations is precious divine work. As members of the human family, each and every one of us holds the store of virtue within our souls that fuels our potential for good. This is something we all share, no matter how deeply hidden it may sometimes be. It is our living, untapped common bond and legacy, and we can begin to tap into it much more actively and effectively as we integrate spirituality and the wisdom at its core in our daily lives. Our relationships with others can thereby grow in true care and respect. Our capacity for empathy is deeply wired, helping us turn toward each other in committed bonds and relationships. This capacity for empathy is first nurtured in the parent-child relationship. Our childhood builds the foundation of our socio-emotional intelligence and social life, while education offers the potential for further development. As we grasp the deeper meaning of our experiences and help those connected with us to understand our insights, we feel safe, seen, and mirrored. We are at home in a world of precious and loving relationships.

The significance of early family relationships for human and societal well-being is well documented in the scientific literature. Riane Eisler, author of many books including the highly acclaimed *The Chalice and the Blade*, raises consciousness of childhood relations as one of the four cornerstones—along with gender equality, enlightened economics, and a collective narrative—in laying the foundation for a new form of democracy that flourishes through people partnering with one another. If we were to consider these four cornerstones deeply in terms of spiritual development, we would emphasize cultivating our capacities for love (in early childhood relationships), harmony (in gender equality), living true purpose (in enlightened economics), and communication (in collective narrative). As Riane Eisler notes, all too often these important facets of life are ignored while measurements like GNP and GDP, military and political dominance, and the quiet submission of poor and marginalized people are considered gauges of a society's success. But Eisler's four cornerstones of a caring democracy are much more aligned with the true peace spiritual development brings, not just measured by, but present in the visible manifestations of love, harmony, true purpose, and enhanced communication. Riane Eisler and I agree that a strong and healthy family unit is foundational to these goals.

Light giving has allowed me an unexpected deep realization of the significance of family relationships and cultivation of the capacity to love and care by living closely, not only early in life, but throughout the lifespan. One evening I was walking by myself after receiving the first day of three days of teachings of the advanced Sukyo Mahikari course in the hot spring-rich, mountainous ancient town of Takayama in Japan. My spirit was soaring after a whole day of absorbing pure teachings at Suza. The evening air was fresh and clear as the Hida River gurgled by. High vibrations of pure love, harmony, and joy filled my heart, having been poured into me through the teachings of the advanced course all day. I was relishing the moment as I walked alone by the river.

As I continued to reflect on the wisdom I had received throughout the day, thoughts of God-centered families in which family members lived closely together and nurtured each other's spiritual development throughout the lifespan began arising within me. I could perceive that in such closely connected families, wisdom can flow naturally through the generations. Family functions of mutual learning and mutual support (of older to younger generations and younger to older generations) in fulfilling true life purpose can be naturally fulfilled throughout the lifespan. My vision had some similarities to my experience of the family in my childhood in India, but this new revelation that came to me as I walked along the river's edge was much further developed and had the power and depth of a foundation of active, family spiritual practice. I began to see that the natural support systems of the intergenerational family unit have been largely dismantled with the advancing influence of materialism since the industrial era. It's become the norm for offspring to move where the work is or where the money is. But more important than wealth or prestige, the strength of families can be reclaimed and strengthened on a foundation of spiritual development and divine principles. This approach builds spiritual connection with place—a sense of home—and deep roots in the family through which true purpose or mission is naturally fulfilled through divine arrangements. In my mind's eye, I could clearly see the stability, strength, flourishment, and true happiness of healthy, God-centered or spirit-centered family systems reemerging.

I reflected on my adult life, much of which has been lived half a world away from where I was born. My life's path was unknowingly influenced by a partly material-centered family model arising from educational and institutional cultures of my time and level of consciousness. I thought of the teaching I had read in the Sukyo Mahikari prayer book on the cycle of life that says "God has arranged for all things in the universe to make progress by undergoing the processes of gathering and scattering, separating and uniting, and of prospering and declining." I reflected on my growing children and the opportunity we now have to make a U-turn to a God-centered way of life. I was energized and uplifted by the divine wisdom I received.

The next morning, during the second day of the advanced course, unbeknownst to me, teachings on the God-centered family were to be transmitted. That's when I realized that I had experienced a preview of them the previous evening as I walked alone by the Hida River. I took this precious spiritual nourishment deeply to heart.

I found that giving and receiving True Light brings clarity and deepens my empathy with myself, others, and nature, making priceless moments of connection both commonplace and very precious—a process that helps make the world a more comfortable home for more of us. For me, reflection and dialogue in attuned relationships are valuable and necessary complements to the practice of True Light and universal principles, to elevating my mind and developing its capacities for deep empathy, instinct, insight, inspiration, and intuition. As my mind purifies and elevates toward true harmony with God, I move toward experiencing life through my spiritual eye, the window of my soul. I harmonize spiritually with vibrations of great peace. I see divinity in myself, others, and nature. I endeavor to relate to all authentically and with care. I glimpse this direction and condition to be our common human destiny.

In my career as a professor of clinical psychology, I have seen damage done to infants and children and by adults to one another in family systems.

I have appreciated deeply that such situations can be greatly improved by building psychological resiliency and learning to cultivate spiritual awareness, the reflective mind, and selflessness. And my family, like any family, has not been immune to societal strains—in our case, cultural and personal damage caused by displacement, divorce, and the demands of the material-first world. Nonetheless, and on balance, we have been blessed with many wondrous opportunities to grow and give. As I share some of my experiences and deep insights I've discovered with each of my children as we grow together sharing the practice of receiving and giving True Light, I do so with a wider lens on what the family unit means to the culture and world at large. Of course I know my own family best, but I share these stories as a way to explore how spiritual practice both affects and is affected by family life.

Nurturing the Family Nurtures the World

My daughter Mira was six years old, my son Ives was nine, and my eldest son Rudy was sixteen when I received my holy omitama in 2002, thus beginning in earnest my deep commitment to spiritual development. Ten years later (in 2012) Rudy's friend Santanov moved to Los Angeles and came to live with us for two years as he and Rudy co-founded their solar energy company. Santanov quickly joined our family and I consider him one of my children too. The stories of these four young people are in many ways more compelling than anything I or my colleagues and peers can share. They hold the promise of the future in their hands. Their awareness is astounding and, at times, a great burden for them to bear. And so, it is my prayer that they be blessed to receive every opportunity to cultivate through spiritual practice the same elevation of mind that they wish for the planet.

My two youngest children were in elementary school when I first began my journey with Sukyo Mahikari. Monday was a day when Ives and Mira's school had a shorter day, so I organized my schedule at the university to pick them up from school and go to the Pasadena Sukyo Mahikari Center with them before returning home. Thus they began visiting the center regularly and receiving Light every week and I began practicing at the center, giving and receiving Light with whomever was at the center when we arrived. So for Ives and Mira, spiritual practice was a normal part of life, like soccer practice and piano lessons for many children. Of course, they also engaged in sports and music and other extracurricular activities, but receiving Light was part of their life from a young age. Rudy was a bit older when he began receiving Light, but it is clear to me that his early childhood development was crucial in preparing him for a life of service to God. And the blessing of welcoming a fourth "child" into the family fold after Santanov's parents passed away, illustrates for me in the deepest way that we are truly one human family, placed in family pods by divine arrangement.

As the mother of three biological children, witnessing and participating in the birth process, early childhood development, and maturation to adulthood for each of these extraordinary human beings has been one of my life's deepest honors. God's presence in birth, as in death, is made known in ways even people for whom spirituality is a low priority can plainly see. Early childhood experiences have a profound impact on the individual lives that make up societies, as even the pope asked Dan Siegel to explain why looking into our mother's eyes as an infant is so important to our human development. And so, with Riane Eisler's inspired work in mind, I too emphasize the importance of recognizing the central role these deeply personal, often unspoken childhood and family experiences play in developing a more caring, spiritually-grounded, God-centered society.

We each have a family that has shaped our lives in significant ways. More significant than any college degree or professional accomplishment, healthy families rooted in loving care and bonded in spiritual unity are the bedrock foundation of all societies. Yet, the value and importance of family life has been largely left out of the conversation on society's social, economic, and spiritual development. As I share the stories of my children's early lives, I invite you to reflect on the stories that have shaped your life and your loved ones' lives.

Rudy Sets His Sights on the Sun

Rudy was born in Provo, Utah where his father and I had been visiting university faculty for a year. When I was expecting Rudy, I was also teaching my first graduate class at the university. I recall that during a break in one class the students were hovered around a newscast. We soon learned that the space shuttle Challenger had blown up with its crew. As we regrouped and I continued to lecture I realized I was bleeding. At the doctor's office a little later the ultrasound revealed a blood clot over the fetus. The doctor encouraged me to rest, without giving me any guarantees or hope that I would be able to carry the baby to term. I went home and took to bed. The bleeding stopped after a day. Thankfully, the pregnancy progressed and when it was time to deliver the baby I had a very long labor of nearly a day and a half. The umbilical cord was tied tightly around the baby's neck and thus the process of being born was literally strangling him. The presence of a very patient, devoted, and competent doctor, the blessings of Rudy's paternal grandparents in India and mine at my side, the support of Rudy's father Suby, and my younger sister Ruma, and cooperation between Rudy and me eventually led to a healthy, natural birth. That evening Suby said he saw the most glorious sunset of his life. This pure-hearted response to Rudy's birth, upon reflection, revealed to me Rudy's earliest connection with the sun. The next would come four years later, following his father's and my divorce and my moving with Rudy to Pasadena.

While living in Pasadena, Rudy and I loved to spend our afternoons in Tournament Park, a historic park in the area located within the grounds of

California Institute of Technology (Caltech). It was a small, cozy park just right for very young children, with a whole international community of young children and parents there. So, every day after university for me, and Montessori school for him, Rudy and I went to Tournament Park to play in the sand pit and on the jungle gym. So Rudy's first playground in Pasadena was at Caltech, where I learned one day as we were playing that Stephen Hawking would be giving a lecture. Since I was a single mother and had no babysitter available, I took Rudy with me as I went to listen that evening. The audience was spilling out from the auditorium so there were loudspeakers broadcasting the lecture on the lawns outside. I thought it best to be outside as Rudy was only four. So we sat down and began listening to the talk that Stephen Hawking was giving through his computer-assisted voice device. I was amazed to see how deeply serene Rudy was as he listened. He did not move at all until the lecture was over. I leaned over and asked him, "Rudy, what did Stephen Hawking say?" Rudy replied, "He said in fifty million years the sun will go 'boom'!"

And so, Rudy's connections to Caltech and solar energy began to manifest. I could not see it or recognize it, not being a Light giver at that time. These stories simply struck me as a wonderful series of experiences, but I didn't realize the God-given meaning in them that lit the path of Rudy's mission and destiny. I connected the dots only after I began giving Light and began to experience the elevation of my mind. I have thus long wanted to emphasize, if only I could find the words, that every child's purpose is magical and useful as it is God-given, no matter how hidden it may appear to be. If every parent can be helped to see and hear it, they will be better equipped to support and guide their children. If everyone's connection with God would be revived in daily life, in education, and institutions, how much simpler and how much more powerful the path to true happiness in society would be for each life and family?

Rudy was in high school when I first began receiving Light. He was driving at that point and would come on his own to the Pasadena Center to receive

Light very often when my younger children and I were also there. He also went with me to Japan on my first visit to Suza for a Spring Grand Ceremony. Two events occurred in my family soon after I received my holy omitama, both relating to our spiritual elevation. First, my father was diagnosed with cancer. This resulted in my going to India and being there for a month, giving him and my mother Light and helping my father recover from surgery. He recovered well and my parents had seven good years after that. Second, during this time when I was in India for my father's surgery, Rudy's college entrance results began coming in and he received acceptance at Caltech, which is about three miles from our home and about four miles from the Pasadena Center. He accepted this offer and continued to go to the Pasadena Center throughout college.

At Caltech he felt the education was a challenge he was up for, but he also found it not well-rounded at the time, with its overemphasis on the hard sciences and its majority male student body. Nonetheless, he persevered with great heart. His basketball coach at Caltech recognized Rudy's perseverance displayed on the court. At first, none of us could fathom why, when tennis was his strong game, he would choose to play basketball at Caltech. "Where else could I play on a college basketball team?" was his response. This was classic Rudy, always broadening himself and seeking out opportunities to grow. He has always embraced life's challenges with gusto.

Two experiences during Rudy's college days stand out in my memory. Though he did not care that much for the science and engineering courses, in his social entrepreneurship class where he was given the opportunity to use technology to help raise the quality of life of disadvantaged people, he came alive and became a leader. He loved that class and formed a deep relationship with the professor that continues to this day. In that class he led a team that designed a low-cost wheelchair made from bicycle parts that received recognition and a prize from Popular Mechanics magazine. With funds from various sources, Rudy and his team established a non-profit company called Intelligent Mobility

International (IMI) while still undergraduate students at Caltech. IMI began an operation in Guatemala and continued for several years. It could be said that this experience changed the course of Rudy's life, but I see it more as a continuation of the divine mission he was born to develop.

Rudy had another transformative experience at Caltech while leading a team in a Stirling engine design competition. Despite great efforts by all on the team, they could not get their engine to work. Rudy called David at home the night before the competition, after having done his utmost with his team. David, hearing the whole grueling story, advised Rudy to simply tell the story of their failure and what they had learned from it. Crestfallen, Rudy accepted defeat and hoped for the best. The next morning as he awaited the arrival of the judges—who were reputable leaders in their fields from outside the university—Rudy was ready to present his failure speech. As the team set up and their judge, who was a renowned entrepreneur, came up to them, the engine started up for the first time! Rudy dropped his failure speech and gave a totally different talk on the spot. When he graduated Caltech, Rudy accepted a job at a solar energy start-up at this same entrepreneur's incubator in Pasadena.

A year later he wanted to take his grandparents (my parents) on a holiday with his first earnings. My parents had come to Pasadena for the summer and planned to go with Rudy to Rome and Pompeii on their way back to India. It was one evening during that summer when I was giving Rudy Light to his main soul in our dining room that I felt an especially high and sacred attunement. As Rudy opened his eyes after receiving Light he said, "I want to learn to give Light." That summer Rudy received the primary course and his holy omitama at the Pasadena Center before leaving for Italy. My father's health deteriorated on that trip, and a year and a half later, when he passed away, Rudy was with him in India and carried out his last rites.

Rudy continued to harmonize at the Pasadena Center and as he traveled for his work he visited Sukyo Mahikari centers all over the world. Being gregarious by nature, he told people of our Light giving practice often. People thus came to receive Light and some received holy omitama. Soon Rudy's life changed from being a solar energy start-up company employee to becoming a solar energy start-up company co-founder. The ups and downs of Rudy's life, the life of his company, and our family life might be the subject of his own book one day. But, for the purposes of this book, I can attest to what I have witnessed: at all times and facing every kind of adversity, the Light, guidance, and protection of God have been ever present in Rudy's life.

I recall leaving the Pasadena Center with Rudy one morning after exchanging Light. As we were leaving, Rudy looked at his cell phone and found an extraordinary invitation from a member of the President's Energy Council who was offering him his $50,000 seat on a ship to Antarctica with Robert Swan, the polar explorer of the 2041 Foundation. A small group of renewable energy executives were planning to journey to Antarctica together to raise each other's consciousness on preserving the earth. Rudy asked me if he should go. I encouraged him strongly. Soon we were getting him organized to head to Ushuaia in Argentina to board his ship. So he went to the seventh continent. There among his adventures was the experience of accidentally falling into an ice hole, which was to be avoided at all costs as survival time in such a hole was very short. As soon as he found himself in the hole, he said he immediately relaxed knowing that his teammates would save him. They did. They pulled him out unharmed.

Another chapter in his life story began unfolding several years ago. Rudy sustained an injury when a box fell on his back when Santanov and he were moving some boxes in their office. Sciatica pains followed and were relieved by the care of a very gifted osteopathic physician (DO). A few years later, his lower back sustained stress again when a bus he was traveling in met with an accident. Again treatment relieved him. Then, when Ives was accepted to a graduate program in architecture at Yale, Rudy, David, Ives, and I set out for their open house in Connecticut. Just as we were leaving on this trip, Rudy woke up one morning, stretched, and experienced the greatest pain he had ever felt in his life. It was in his neck. Two reputable conventional orthopedic surgeons declared the situation very serious and recommended surgery, which itself, they said, could be very dangerous and involve a very long convalescence. After his second consultation Rudy called me and said, "This is not aligned, Mom." I was so deeply grateful to hear his realization, for I too realized its truth immediately and supported him wholeheartedly. Rudy knew that his doctors were practicing material-first standard medicine and he knew even more deeply as he stood on an inner precipice with a potentially very debilitating health condition that this guidance was not aligned with divine will and principles, with taking care of his spirit, mind, and body as a totality.

We went back to the DO together. She was also deeply concerned and worked with him with her hands for the equivalent of about three sessions that first day, staying with us late into the night. She explained that the earlier stresses to Rudy's lower back had made his neck vulnerable and, given his relentless pace of work, it gave way. She prescribed regular osteopathic adjustments with a whole range of additional practices such as yoga, Qi gong, dietary supplements, and more.

Rudy was committed and diligent in following the guidance. He continued to give and receive Light and learned to slow the pace of his life. His workday remains long, though he travels much less now. After more than two years, his scans, doctor evaluations, and experience show that, by God's grace, he is improving. Recently, he began weekly service at the Sukyo Mahikari center and we hope he will steadily overcome this purification related to this injury.

Now, as we close in on a decade since its founding, by God's blessing, Santanov and Rudy's solar energy company (which is named HST) has not only survived but is thriving. It is a singular honor for Santanov and Rudy, HST, and our family to participate in the renewable energy revolution. One day Rudy hopes to return to the type of philanthropic work he did with IMI in college, which is also something he has in his heart to do. Rudy has been called by God to bring love and harmony to the world. But first, it seems, he must allow the greater goal of harmony to manifest in his own spirit, mind, and body. I believe strongly that God has given Rudy a spiritual mission, through which he and I together have had many highs and lows of precious purification. His soul is pure and luminous and he loves to give and receive Light. Not long ago, he went to see his father in Kolkata, India and offered to give Light to him, which Suby has not, as of yet, been willing to receive. We hope this will change as Rudy becomes stronger in his divine service and practice.

When Rudy was born, I felt a sense of empowerment. This firstborn son of the Roy family brought a new generation of the Roy lineage to the world, which is very important in Indian culture and in many cultures around the world. At that time I did not realize that this was part of my divine mission, too, and that there was further to go to help that descendant fulfill his destiny. Unconsciously, I had a vague sense of the elevation needed. The journey forward was emotionally torturous, which would have been greatly ameliorated and more filled with amity and joy had I already been permitted to give Light then.

I hope with all of my heart that spiritual development and awakening can grow in parents and families throughout the lifespan so that their service to God and others may progress in the best conditions. This, in my experience, becomes possible as we actively serve God with joy, erase the spiritual impurities every single one of us has, and live in tune with the divine principles.

Recently Rudy asked me when the next intermediate spiritual development course might give him an opportunity to elevate his omitama. I pray he will be allowed to do so in the near future, and I pray he is allowed to fulfill the step of offering dedicated weekly center service at the Pasadena Sukyo Mahikari Center. He is being allowed to make effort toward this step now. Every small step for God is a big step for a person, their ancestors, and their whole family—

so deeply interconnected are our relationships in all three worlds of the divine, astral, and physical. I also pray that my aspiration to receive Goshintai—the holy scroll through which people can harmonize themselves with God—and to establish a home Light giving center is fulfilled soon, united with my family with one of my children as my helper. May Rudy (the inventor) and Ives (the architect) be called to co-create in both their professional and spiritual lives.

Building Momentum with Ives

My second child, Ives, was born in Pasadena. His first action as a newborn was to turn his head to take a good look around the room. Ives was born ready to connect with the world! He was awake, serene, and his neck was strong, fully able to support his head. Indeed, he was fully present as he took his first breath.

Ives was always a very cheerful child who adored his older brother Rudy. Rudy had said to me when I began expecting Ives that he needed a brother, so I am so happy Ives came along when he did! When their sister Mira arrived, Ives and Rudy and she all became the best of friends. All of the children love to be with each other. It gives me great joy to witness how they inspire and nurture each other.

By the time Ives was a young boy his fine-motor skills allowed him to draw expressively, pouring his creative inspiration beautifully on to the page. Attentively and deftly drawing family and nature, when he was about four years old he drew a bright, colorful cubist portrait of a person with a walrus on their head. The person's mouth was crooked and placed on the side of the face. Curious to know why, I asked him. He replied, "If you have a walrus on your head your mouth will be crooked." A keen observer of human experience from early on, he could represent his empathy on paper and even as a toddler he would be immersed in building large, intricate, beautiful, stable structures with wooden blocks. As they came together he would clap his hands with joy.

He also manifested the selflessness and nonattachment I had seen in my family in India early in my life. One year when he realized it was my birthday he ran back to his room, rummaged through his box of special things and took out a two dollar note keepsake, all the money he had in the world and gifted it to me with a big smile.

Yet again I did not connect the dots, seeing only his talents and inclinations rather than his soul's connections. Without spiritual practice and elevation of mind I could not yet see deeply his way to architecture or his heart of giving, which is also the heart of service. After I became a Light giver when Ives was nine years old, we received a mysterious and most wonderful arrangement. I had signed Ives and Mira up for a summer art program at the nearby Norton Simon Museum on the theme of Hiroshige's wood blocks. When it came time to show up I called to confirm details and found that neither Ives nor Mira had been enrolled. I was taken aback only for a moment as the education coordinator quickly assured me that there was something even better available for them, a new program by a renowned trio of two architects and an urban planner who had volunteered to work in small teams with youth to re-envision Hollywood and present their work at a public reception at Los Angeles Contemporary Exhibitions (LACE). Ives and Mira were enthusiastic to participate and from then on, through this and many other wonderful opportunities in the US and in India, Ives began to connect with the field of architecture, a God-given gift.

In school, Ives liked the order in mathematics and could work with it with ease. He liked the creative freedom in art and physics even more. Yet this was not enough. He wanted to use his abilities to make a tangible difference in peoples' lives. This he found in architecture because he found it to be a living field, something people are in constant interaction with. Something that emanates meaning, creates a social climate, and is in turn influenced by it. As Ives has said, architecture is the "way a structure becomes a home, and those who live inside become a family." Thus, architecture balances for him the sensations found in physics and art and embodies what he felt was lacking: something for people to identify with and a context for the progression of society.

Ives draws on the two worlds he occupies, the United States of America and India, as he navigates life. He carries within him the experience of his home in Pasadena, situated in a context that places high value on privacy and individual autonomy and lower value on collective public spaces. He feels that creating infrastructure with pure utilitarian intention—as is often the case in many modern, urban environments—creates cultures of separation and stratification. Ives envisions the sterility that often accompanies convenience being replaced by interaction and vibrancy. At the same time, he turns to ecological data, research, and net-zero environmentally sustainable building practices to provide some of the agency in his design and development. He also draws both by hand and digitally to bring to life his sensibility for harmony between built and natural ecologies.

At the same time, Ives carries within him the experience of his grandparents' home in Noida, outside New Delhi, India. He has been awestruck since he was a young child by how each parcel of public land is exhaustively occupied, even by farm animals. As a toddler, when he landed at the New Delhi airport and was driven home by my parents, he would be overjoyed to spot cows and buffalos on the road. His grandfather (my father) would take him for evening neighborhood drives to see more urban livestock as Ives was so filled with joy by their meandering presence through the streets. Thus he realized that strong, diverse communities in densely populated environments with cultures of informal relationships can facilitate healthy, rich environments for people to come together and grow together.

In India, Ives spent a lot of time playing sports with informal groups assembled at the park. Numerous people, family and friends, visited his grandparents' ground floor apartment each day. One of his most poignant memories of human contact in Noida Ives experienced while drawing in his sketchbook at the park in the afternoons. During these times, a different young child would always come over to see what he was doing, and sometimes put their arm around him and watch him draw. Such curiosity and open embrace of a stranger in a public park was something Ives only experienced in India. He later learned that many of his friends in the park were the children of people who worked for middle-class families and lived in the same neighborhood in their helpers' quarters. It was in these fundamentally warm, spontaneous, cross-strata connections with people that Ives experienced and felt how a city can bring people together.

In an early undergraduate project at UCLA, Ives responded to emerging policies to regulate informal micro-economies such as fruit stands, food stands, food trucks, and street vendors by designing open-air architectural typologies per block to act as loose containers for informal markets and public parks, lifting housing and office programs on an infrastructure above. Since then, to this day, in his present graduate advanced studio on development and architecture at Yale, in which he is reimagining and repurposing an old navy shipyard to provide workspaces to expand economic opportunities in the community, Ives continues to be guided in his responses by his connection with the world and his inherent selflessness and humanity. His serenity and joy guide his inspiration as he grows as a person striving to bring harmony to the experience of others.

Ives has received Light since he was nine years old. He was always cheerful at the Pasadena Sukyo Mahikari Center, where he and one of the staff members would play baseball in the parking lot after Light giving. When Ives was in high school this staff member married a former staff member at Suza. They were the sweetest, most gentle, lovely couple. Ives somehow heard of this wedding being conducted at the Los Angeles Center and wanted to attend. So he and I attended our first Sukyo Mahikari wedding together!

Ives had been a leader in high school, both in the classroom and on the playing fields. Going from initially shaking in utter fear on the pitcher's mound when asked to pitch on his high school baseball team, he went on to pitch the first no-hitter in school history. He also connected with members of the Sukyo Mahikari Pasadena Center who were practicing 4Rs (Reduce, Reuse, Recycle, and Repair) and was inspired to action. Gathering up two close friends, he founded the Green Club at his large public high school. They brought recycling into the school and joined forces with the City of Pasadena to help the club earn revenue through recycling, which it began doing in a substantial way.

Throughout high school, Ives seemed happy to receive Light, but he didn't say anything about giving Light. So, at one point when he was an undergrad at UCLA, I asked him about it and he seemed mixed in his response. I had gone to India and on my return I found that Ives was suffering some discrimination at the hands of a professor. After helping him with his own coping and discussing departmental redress, I told him about the deeper, personal aspect of spiritual purification and encouraged him to receive the primary course. About a month later, he did, along with Santanov. As Ives began to give Light, the negative experiences he had been having began to decrease. The professor seemed to move out of his life and Ives began to realize the spiritual truth of the guidance I had been allowed to give him.

At UCLA, Ives found his way to the architecture department and almost immediately began paying attention to sustainable building practices. My father once said that if he had to do it over again, he would be an architect. So, when Ives found architecture I smiled. As I mentioned earlier, I recently had the inspiration that we could build a small holy Goshintai building in our backyard as our family offering to God and Ives' first commission as an architect. I brought Rudy, Ives, and Mira together and shared this idea. Everyone immediately unified joyously. Later when I mentioned it to David he opened up to it as well. And so, this project is something that Ives and I are working on with David, Rudy, Mira, and the Pasadena Center's support.

Before graduating from UCLA, Ives organized a Sukyo Mahikari Open House with the Mindfulness Club at UCLA, which was the student chapter of the Mindfulness Awareness Research Center (MARC) founded by Dan Siegel and another UCLA psychiatry professor named Sue Smalley, whom I once had the privilege to welcome and give Light to at the Pasadena Center. At the open house, a Sukyo Mahikari staff member introduced the practice, Ives talked about his and his family's practice, and then we invited everyone to receive Light. Several Light givers who were UCLA alumni, David, and I attended. About twenty UCLA students from the Mindfulness Club participated. After Light giving, we all sat in a circle and I facilitated a reflection group. It was wonderful. And since the desire to repeat the experience was expressed, we did the same program again the following year.

When Ives graduated UCLA, he took a job at a small architecture firm in Pasadena that was focused on environmentally-conscious net zero footprint projects in schools and houses. Almost immediately, he got the chance to work on such a project within his own old school district in Pasadena. He also offered divine service at the Pasadena Center with me on a weekly basis. That same year, Ives went to Suza with David and me and participated with us in the Yokatta-ne or Seeds of Light dance on the grand stage of Suza. Along with practitioners from all over Los Angeles, we had prepared for many months with the guidance of staff, choreographers and orchestras at our centers, praying, giving and receiving Light together, and practicing our dances. It was both intense and joyful, and we all bonded with one another through the ups and downs involved in being part of a theatrical production. On the day of the performance great energy and joy emanated through us to the audience and from them back to us. Somewhere in the middle of the dance I noticed that people from the farthest corners of the grand hall (which held ten thousand people) to the dignitaries in the front row were standing up, waving handkerchiefs, and dancing with us. Indeed, the audience left Suza smiling, still dancing and filled with joy.

A couple of years later, Ives went to Suza again on his own steam to attend the Spring Grand Ceremony. Then he applied to graduate school and accepted an offer at Yale. But before he went away to school, he connected with a renowned Indian architect in New Delhi and got a summer job working with him in the Himalayas. This architect is known for pushing the envelope for solutions to water shortage issues through innovations in reclaiming water from river sand banks and planning small, ecologically natural cities. And so, Ives went to India to help him design some homes he was building near Dharamshala.

While living at the foot of the Dhauladhar mountains in the Himalayas, Ives made friends in the community, including with a very old friend of mine, Radhika, who lived nearby with her husband Alain. Ives played soccer in the park and settled down to work. One day, while riding pillion on a friend's motorbike to get lunch, another motorbike ran into them. Everyone was thrown off, but no one was hurt except Ives, whose right ankle was bleeding profusely. People were gathering and wanting to help. He did not want anyone to touch his wound and he wanted the right advice on which hospital to go to. He was getting overwhelmed and about to pass out when his phone rang. It was my mother calling from the New Delhi area hundreds of miles away. She insisted he call his employer which he then did. Ives' employer kindly showed up, took him to the right hospital, and called Radhika. By the time Radhika called me, Ives was being wheeled in for surgery.

Ives had ruptured his Achilles tendon by eighty percent on his right leg. He was in good spirits though, and Radhika took amazing care of him, communicating with all the doctors and me. I felt totally at ease throughout this time. Radhika's presence was like my own in so very many ways that our teamwork across the globe gave me full confidence in everything and made me feel like I was there. Again, by God's great grace, this had been a profound divine arrangement. I had reconnected with Radhika just a year before after nearly forty years. We had studied psychology together at Lady Shri Ram College in New Delhi and, like me, she was also the daughter of a general. In fact, she was a member of one of the most distinguished families of generals the Indian Army has had. She has a great spark and a deep spiritual practice rooted in the missions of Sri Aurobindo and the Mother of Pondicherry and Auroville. Again, by God's grace, a renowned surgeon and a wonderful person carried out Ives' surgery. Ives did well and in a couple of days my niece Amba flew up from New Delhi to bring him back by airplane for his convalescence in my mother's home in Noida, outside New Delhi. My mother kept Ives very well cared for six weeks, during which time the two very much enjoyed each other's company. He often exchanged Light with my sister Shouma and other Light givers in the area. Amba and her close friends visited him to play board games. He recouped slowly and steadily, though his rehabilitation was long. When he returned to California, Mira and I helped him with his appointments and exercises and, finally, he was off to Yale on crutches. Ives still has a big protruding bump on his right heel, though he can walk without a limp now, and even run without pain. A patient person by nature, he was given the chance to grow much more patient and much more grateful through this purification.

This patience and gratitude were soon put to the test when, in his studio architecture class at Yale last spring, he received neither the professor nor the partner he had chosen. A bit disappointed, he decided to make the best of it with the hope he would be pleasantly surprised. Then, at a crucial point in their project, his partner simply stopped showing up. After reaching out to her repeatedly, he finally learned that she had suddenly lost her closest friend and was deeply grief stricken. She did not want to drop out of classes or delay her program, nor did she want to work on this very challenging assignment on her own. Ives encouraged her to seek counseling, and then he set up a meeting for both of them with their professor. That's when a couple of Ives' friends invited him to join their project, which appealed to him greatly. This gave Ives another idea: perhaps his partner could be reassigned to a project with two of her friends in order to give her the extra personal support she needed at this time. She was open to it and their professor thought it might be a good solution. But the professor in charge of the other group felt it was too late in the semester to make this change, so Ives' partner would be left without a project team. Although Ives still had the option of joining his friends' team, he resolved to stay with his original partner because he felt it would be cruel to abandon her in this time of grief. His partner was very grateful and worked hard as she was able.

Ives' professor said that she knew few people in the competitive environment at Yale architecture school who would have foregone looking out for themselves and made the call Ives did. Perhaps his own injury and surgery that caused him to commence graduate school on crutches had increased his capacity for compassion for his classmates. Soon they would all face new challenges. Just before the COVID-19 pandemic, Ives came home to Pasadena for his spring break. His project partner, who was just beginning to cope with the adversities in her life, had a host more challenges to deal with—being an international student who had to make her way back home in a global pandemic. Ives carried all the extra load on the project, with no resentment of his partner, but genuinely appreciating the strengths she had been able to bring when she could.

At review time something magical happened. A renowned architect from Los Angeles who had not been on Ives' list of reviewers the previous day when he had checked on it and who had reviewed him at UCLA when he was an undergrad, showed up—as if from nowhere—just for Ives and his partner's review. She gave them one of the few rave reviews that day! It was remarkable. Ives felt affirmed that what he and his partner had done on the project, as well as how he had navigated the challenges that arose had been right, in tune with divine will and principles. He was profoundly grateful for this deep inside-out chance to grow in humility, which has come to be Ives' signature leadership style.

Santanov Joins the Family

A shared passion for solar energy brought another future Light giver into our family. Santanov and Rudy met at a solar energy conference held at Harvard. Santanov is from India and is a Bengali like Rudy and me. His full name (Santanobho) is a Bengali name which means "new peace", fittingly and in true alignment with the teachings of a new spiritual civilization and an era of peace on earth emerging from spirit-centered citizens. Santanov came to the US at age sixteen to attend Yale as an undergraduate and, after graduation, entered Harvard Business School. During this time he lost his father to cancer, and at the time Rudy met him, his mother had become a cancer patient also. Rudy mentioned the Light to him and Santanov expressed openness to it. Back in Pasadena, Rudy put Santanov on the phone to me. His first word remains clearly in my mind: he called me "Aunty." Although this is not an unusual address among Indians, I was taken aback and touched by the warmth and closeness in the tone of his address. He put me in contact with his mother, Rina, in Kolkata, India. I began calling her and speaking with her, making friends and giving Light to her indirectly by speaking with her. There was just one person in Kolkata who could give Light and it was quite a challenge for Rina to meet with her, despite the desire on both sides to connect.

Very soon, however, Santanov arrived in our home, a bright, cheerful, magical young man. Santanov told Rudy that my appearance and attitudes were surprisingly like his mother's. Even her name rhymes with mine. When Rudy and he decided to start a solar energy company together, their work, adventures, and trials began in our home. Our entire family embraced the founding of HST and supported them in the start-up process thoroughly. I continued to speak with Santanov's mother, Rina, and began giving him Light and taking him to the Pasadena Center. Within a short time, while Santanov was in Italy on a business trip, he received news that his mother had suddenly passed away. He and his younger brother Anurag, who was in the United States at the time, reached India just in time for the last rites. When Santanov returned to Pasadena, our home truly became his home.

But Santanov's grieving heart took some time to settle in. He deposited his large suitcase in a corner of his room and lived out of it instead of unpacking his clothes and belongings like a member of the family. Over time, his pile of laundry and belongings became larger and more unkempt. I gently encouraged him to keep his things in a closet, offering to help him organize his belongings. He was quick to say he would do it himself, but he never seemed to get around to it. Through my psychologist's eye, I saw that huge lump in the corner of the room as a manifestation of his great grief. I realized that unpacking his suitcase was an action that would, in some subconscious way, finalize his parents' deaths, and so I treated him especially gently with it. One day, in a moment of clarity, I felt it was time to move forward and asked him if we could unpack and organize his things together. At first, he insisted he would do it himself as he had numerous times before and then, realizing that I really wanted it done, he quietly followed me to his room where we slowly unpacked all his things and arranged them nicely.

It went smoothly until the end, when Santanov's resistance surfaced and he complained "Now I feel like a baby."

"It's all in your attitude," I replied. "You could be feeling like a prince."

Always bright and open, Santanov made a visible U-turn in his attitude as he smiled brightly, uplifted in spirit, and said "That's true."

It took eight months for Santanov to unpack his bags and settle in as a member of our family. Even though he was a young professional with two Ivy

League degrees and a successful solar energy start-up underway, he needed to be embraced by people who consider him family and love him for who he is. We all need this. It's interesting to me that it took almost as long as the human gestation period for this fourth child of mine to truly arrive. He has blessed our family with his presence, his love, and his willingness to receive our love.

Soon after, Santanov and Ives both received their holy omitama. Santanov learned the prayer of purification and pronounced it clearly and correctly like all my children. Sometimes he attended study classes at the Pasadena Center with David and me, including one on the construction of Suza that was given at that time. He sat reverently with us as we inaugurated a new ancestor tablet in the Brown family ancestor altar for David's mother after she passed away. HST was in its very early stages then. Santanov had to travel up north to a small Californian town to set up some solar racks. He took his omitama with him and accidentally returned without it. The Center Director asked him to write an apology to God which he did sincerely in long hand from his heart with an offering. He received a new omitama.

Many a year on a holiday such as Christmas day, when I offered some service at the Pasadena Center behind closed doors, Santanov would show up to offer service and exchange Light with me. When he and Rudy went to Honolulu for their work, they (along with Mira who was working there at the time) enjoyed meeting Honolulu Center members over lunch and visiting the Honolulu Center. Santanov, who loves the sea, was in high spirits, waking early to go scuba diving and savoring the experience. At the Honolulu Center he, Rudy, and Mira felt very uplifted and Santanov, who has an ease with numbers and finance, had the wish arise in him to help expand the center's prosperity. I pray as Santanov grows in his divine service and practice he will do so. I realize that such desires to repay God are noble desires to repay our divine parent for that which we can never repay. I also realize that our divine service of giving Light, physical service of care of centers, and financial/material offerings are offerings and not donations that we are allowed to make. They become true offerings as the vibration of our innermost attitudes elevate and harmonizes with God's will and we are filled with gratitude, acceptance and humility as we make them.

I often encourage Santanov to give a little Light where he is, every day. He often tells me that he does and I feel the joy he feels when he does. He has numerous friends from all over the world and can really enjoy good times with all of them. Though he loves being home, living at home, working from home, and eating simple, fresh, home-cooked Bengali food with us whenever he is with us. As he grows spiritually to see himself for who he is and grounds himself in God and the divine principles in daily life, I pray that his path home will naturally open up for him in every way.

During the COVID-19 pandemic, Santanov faced a health crisis which necessitated a change in his diet and exercise routine. I reported his situation on his behalf to our group coordinator as he is still learning the significance of such spiritual steps. Our group coordinator gladly and sincerely offered prayers for him. Santanov got to set up wonderful new food arrangements and moved residence to where he could swim every night after his long workday. He made remarkably good progress to renewed health within a few short months and got to appreciate the blessing of his body by taking care of it well.

During the long southern California summer this year, the pipes in Santanov's residence burst, flooding his house on a one-hundred-and-ten-degree day. Panicked by this incident, Santanov called for help. We answered the call and helped him deal with all of his belongings, some of them coming to our house and others to storage until he finds another place to live. It sometimes seems God is in a hurry to move Santanov forward through ups and downs resulting in his spiritual elevation!

It's wonderful to see Santanov's rhythm of divine service evolve. Every small step towards God calls for sincere and true effort, and accomplishing the step reflects spiritual elevation and divine blessing for service at centers, home, and missions in the world. From time to time, Santanov and Rudy give Light to each other, too, and sometimes Santanov reads the holy books of gratitude and the Goseigen. He hopes to travel with us to Suza one day soon. I look forward to that time of deepening our relationship as we experience together the deepening of our spiritual practice.

Mira's Authentic Voice

You've already read the story of my daughter Mira's decision to become a Light giver, which was the beginning of a great spiritual journey for her. Her early and auspicious desire to give Light to young children belies her truly gracious, humble soul and her pure motivation to elevate her mind for the good of all. Initially, Mira wanted to give and receive Light with me alone, though as she matured this changed and she opened up to others. While most people would have described her as a shy child, I always saw her quiet resolve and strength. She was full of surprises. When she was in elementary school, she participated in summer musical theater productions. One summer while performing in a production celebrating Broadway, she belted out a most powerful, poised, and beautiful rendition of the Frank Sinatra song "New York, New York." We were all stunned and amazed to see and hear that she had found her voice.

When Mira was in high school, she was invited by her peers to take leadership of the Green Club, the recycling and environmental action club that Ives had founded. She led with wisdom, fortitude, and a deep sense of inclusiveness, overcoming challenges by depending upon her inner resolve and her bonds with family and true friends. She expanded the recycling program and was passionate about raising her peers' consciousness so that recycling was elevated from a rule followed at school to a way of life inspired by genuine commitment to helping the earth flourish. In this way she was actively practicing the universal principle of reducing waste and treating materials preciously. Under Mira's leadership, the Green Club expanded from the small, committed core group established by her brother, to a large and vibrant membership. The club's financial base grew, and Mira wrote about the club's activities in the school newspaper. The club linked with other organizations inside and outside the city to create broader support for important environmental initiatives, such as tree planting.

As her senior year approached, searching for a legacy contribution, Mira conceived of a garden of native plants. She took the idea to the Green Club membership in her characteristically humble and open manner. The club members enthusiastically owned it! It became everyone's project. Collaborations began with the school administration and other organizations, including a very well-established local foundation that promoted native gardening. A large piece of land within the school grounds was given to the Green Club. The club planted the large garden themselves, with feedback from the professionals at the foundation, choosing and purchasing four hundred plants and ten trees.

A challenge arose when the parents' organization wanted to participate, contribute funds, and, ultimately, take credit for the native garden. The spirit of their engagement was contrary to the true spirit of humility and collaboration at the project's core, which upset Mira deeply. She took time to reflect. At times she shed quiet tears at home; other times she stood up and made her voice heard. At all times she made sense of what was happening, reached for the love and wisdom within her, and communicated harmoniously. I listened and watched her with deep gratitude. I reflected her wisdom back to her and offered her my perspective. She made sense of a particularly painful set of interactions by wisely observing: "I think that when some people's children go to high school, they [the parents] go back to being the way they were in high school too." Making sense of the chaos, she concluded "All that matters is that the work is done, and that is what we must do." With this clarity, Mira at age eighteen overcame the challenges she faced and saw her idea take shape as a permanent gift that raised the environmental consciousness of the school and community.

The day of the native garden's planting felt holy. About fifty people showed up in the quiet of the early morning—students, teachers, parents, administrators and members of like-minded organizations. The scent of donated woodchips and rows and rows of trees and plants ready to be planted tuned everyone's attention to the vibrations of peace on earth, and the human spirit of stewardship, love, harmony, and growth. A volunteer from a like-minded organization suggested that everyone gather in a circle, reminiscent of a native American ceremony, to offer gratitude before planting the garden. All joined hands to offer gratitude and pray to materialize a native garden as part of Mother Earth for the benefit of all.

The group began the work of digging, planting, and mulching in accordance with the garden plan. There was a great self-governed orderliness and diligence as people worked together. Mira and I discreetly offered True Light to the general area—the garden, plants, trees, and volunteers. With a sense of harmony, good humor, and—above all—peace, the garden was planted. This garden began with quiet, resolute, collective action by conscientious youth in a Pasadena public school—a school that had been abandoned by many families when public schools in this very economically privileged community were desegregated decades ago. The garden was a victory for peace, cooperation, and connectivity with all. It continues to shine as a beacon of hope. As a mother, I smile broadly each time I think of this garden.

On a recent visit to her old high school, Mira found the trees in the native garden flourishing, and the Green Club thriving. The Club's latest initiative is a very beautiful organic vegetable garden on campus, supplying some of the produce served at the school cafeteria. This is truly heartwarming! I am immensely grateful that my children have been allowed to integrate spirituality in their daily lives, practice the universal principles, and naturally give to the community.

When Mira set out for college at Cal Poly San Luis Obispo, she kept her omitama with her, and when she had the chance to meet with an elderly lady who lived near her college to exchange Light she did. A couple of years later, a young woman from a longtime Sukyo Mahikari family joined her college. The two of them got together to exchange Light. If either went through minor ailments they reached out to each other to exchange Light and use holistic remedies. When Sukyo Mahikari staff members went out to the area near her college to give Light she had the chance to meet them to receive Light also.

This spiritual foundation helped Mira face adversity away from home with great resolve and courage. Thus she overcame experiences of rampant racism and a materialistic approach to environmental studies (her first major). She became very clear that the environmental science programs she was encountering were oriented toward meeting environmental corporate social responsibility criteria on a relatively surface level. She knew that she did not want to be part of such paths, even though jobs after graduation were supposed to be plentiful. In her social environment in college she had numerous experiences of outright racism in dormitories and on campus. It was her first experience as a brown person in a largely white environment. She had never experienced so much micro-aggression, whether it was out of unawareness, hostility, or a blatantly oppressive attitude. These experiences occurred with her peers, their parents, and her professors.

For example, in one of her first physics classes when she reached out for help the professor's first response was "maybe you ought to choose a different class." Mira reflected and wondered why her first response right off the bat was that and not "Let me see how I can help you?" Why was it "Maybe you do not belong here?" As Mira began listening to the metacommunication, that is, the meaning in the communication, she began to experience her own anger and realized how rampant racism, sexism, majorism, and unexamined prejudice were prevalent in her college environment on personal and institutional levels. She also realized that engaging the anger was not going to be helpful to her life. It was then that a new major and an opportunity to serve as a research assistant appeared in her life and helped her to cope and grow.

Happily settled into her new major, anthropology and geography, Mira took on a research role on an National Science Foundation funded project called Advancing Cultural Change that was raising consciousness on inequities of funding and recognition between majors on campus. The research opportunities opened up an avenue to work closely with a team on focus groups on racism and majorism, which examined the inequities of funding and space given to majors such as engineering and architecture as compared to liberal arts and social sciences, as well as the values and attitudes supporting these resource allocations. This was hard work that was often met with resistance and hostility. The team was strong, though, and committed to their work. They debriefed with each other, worked hard together, made presentations, participated in conferences and continued to find the courage and energy to forge ahead. Mira began to get a real taste for what awareness-raising and empathy-engendering work of discarding materialism, self-centeredness, and internal fragility can look like and feel like as she discovered what it takes to become a social justice advocate. Her spiritual practice and foundation continued to ground her in wisdom and give her strength. These experiences put her on a path of internal growth even more strongly, both spiritually and psychologically. She began to naturally integrate her thoughts and feelings to calmly and clearly see through difficult, painful, inflammatory situations and offer her penetrating insights succinctly, empathically, and objectively. Thus she was growing and training on her path of engaging with others to contribute to a more just and equal world.

This clarity began to show up in Mira's writing. Her words began to carry a true sense of connection and wisdom. At the same time, her handwritten notes in her beautiful handwriting continued to go right to the point in the warmest way. She and her brothers grew up writing letters by hand from time to time, and they also wrote reflections by hand when they had to grasp a lesson. This was something I would do with them when they were young. They continue to write and draw by hand now, for which I am truly grateful, for it carries the message and vibrations of the heart so directly. I grew up with regular letter writing back and forth with family and friends, which kept our relationships so warm, connected, and growing. I have returned to this practice since becoming a Light giver and receive so much appreciation from recipients for the warmth of a handwritten letter. It makes me happy to see that, as comfortable as Mira and her brothers are with navigating technology to communicate, writing by hand remains a part of their lives.

When they were small, my children loved coming to my office to play or have their sick bay there when this had to happen occasionally. Mira was unique in that I took her into my meetings and classroom at least a couple of times between the ages of one to two when I had no alternative. On one occasion, which happened to be my birthday, I spoke at an Asian American Student Conference with her in my arms. Another time it was a three-hour long graduate seminar on self-awareness development. Mira was rapt in her attention and totally angelic on both occasions. As she nestled closely in my arms she was so at home in both situations and later surprised us by using the word "seminar" conversationally as a pre-schooler! Now Mira is part of our Circles project and helps with our evaluation component. Occasionally she joins our Zoom self-training meetings and is friends with all the team members.

When Mira was in preschool, she would spend hours on her own working on complex puzzles and bringing them together. She did them with focus and peace. This intrinsic capacity re-integrated within her as she experienced, coped with, began learning to work with and write about injustice and a path to justice in the world. A journal article she has written with her research team will soon be published in a mainstream anthropology journal. Mira continues to approach most everything she does in her authentic voice, which is inspired yet grounded and carries a sense of connection and justice.

One summer as we were discussing internship possibilities, Mira told me that she knew she needed to work in closely connected relationships. One insight led to another, and she began saving money to found a small pottery project, which she did two years later in a public policy institute and children's school in the Himalayas. We went there together and Mira built relationships with the staff as they organized a pottery wheel, held a pottery workshop with a local potter, and trained two teachers in the afterschool program. They took it up so enthusiastically that they integrated pottery into all their programs for children and youth. Now, as gifted youth from economically disadvantaged schools all over India come through their environmental consciousness raising programs, they all get to do some pottery too.

While Mira waited patiently for her first job out of college to materialize, she interned at her old elementary school where she was a student at the time she first received her holy omitama. She loved working alongside her favorite teacher in her old third grade classroom. The students adored her, a feeling she fully reciprocated. When she was offered a job in Hawaii, she moved to Honolulu, not far from where Rudy and I had lived thirty years prior. Two of my colleagues there had also received their holy omitamas in recent years. When I travelled to Honolulu with Mira to help her get settled into her new place, she and I went to the Sukyo Mahikari center there, met old friends, and went to familiar places. Mira built close connections with the Honolulu Center, went there often, and felt deeply nurtured there. She also joined the pottery guild. In her time living in Hawaii, she learned that she loved to be home with her family, loved the sea, and enjoyed work that spanned the whole range from direct intervention, to research, policy, leadership, and philanthropy.

This is exactly the kind of job she received next. It brought her back home to California and gave her the chance to work on a small team serving at-risk children in the neglected schools of Los Angeles. She currently works on a reading program that concentrates on confidence building and mindfulness as it builds competencies. Mira also gives Light at home and at the Pasadena Center regularly. These days our center is closed due to the COVID-19 pandemic, but we can offer a very special service to take care of the holy objects. Mira, like her brothers, comes to the center each week to train herself spiritually and offer this service with me. Just as it gave me joy on the first day when she decided she would like to learn to give Light, each time she comes to offer divine service at the center gives me joy. When I see her participate in opening prayers at the center, give and receive Light, be inspired to clean a corner of the center, I see her fulfilling a wondrous opportunity of connection for her true self with God. On the days she does not visit the center, Mira usually gives and receives Light at home. As Mira grows, I see the wisdom and clarity within her emerge continually. She discerns, chooses what fits, learns, grows, and receives divine arrangements as she is blessed to practice Light giving and awaken to her relationship with God, little by little.

The Strength of the Intergenerational Family

I see that the deep spiritual awareness we all have as human beings in infancy and early life can most naturally be kept alive and developed in our families by following any genuine spiritual practice in our daily lives. Through such practice, our childlike and childhood purity and power can be kept alive and grown in daily life through our closest relationships, which are some of our most significant God-given treasures. As we turn to these relationships as the valuable life foundation they are, they can be oriented to fulfilling their spiritual, sacred purpose of growing spiritually together. For such fulfillment, daily spiritual practice and face-to-face interactions are necessary, as is the continual effort to elevate innermost attitudes to serve God in the world. When worldly, material knowledge and pursuit are built upon a living spiritual foundation, divine wisdom guides our conscious, discerning engagement and contributions in the world and are in tune with God. This is vital for naturally flourishing in our world today and in the future and for the evolution of our personal lives, fields, and systems in society.

For such great change and spiritual upliftment of all human beings and society, intergenerational families are a strong, natural unit. This is the precious vision I was allowed to experience as I walked by the Hida river in Takayama, Japan. At the time, I was filled with the divine vibrations of God emanating from the teachings of the advanced course at the World Shrine, Suza. These had been transmitted all day for the first of three days of the advanced spiritual development course. I realized that the purpose of this spiritual action is true happiness, stability, and harmony in the small spheres of homes synergistically reflected on to the large sphere of the world and the earth. This is something we can evolve into, one catalytic step at a time.

The experience of direct connection with God reconnects us with our first and eternal relationship, that of our soul with God. Daily spiritual practice and a context and culture of spiritual practice with our families creates a true home for this first relationship. We naturally harmonize with the divine will and principles and recognize our soul's infinite path of development. Our minds, bodies, and material lives gain a foundation and framework on which to grow spiritually toward a peaceful, spiritual future for the human family and the earth.

Our spiritual actions free us from falling off dangerous precipices of our own making, be it destruction of the environment or long histories of conflict and antagonism undertaken for material security and advancement without attunement to divine principles. Our spiritual actions also free us from endlessly circumperambulating the base of the mountain (so to speak) by living lives of material-centered, self-centered awareness. We can make a U-turn to elevate to spirit-centeredness through true spiritual paths and by daily practice with the sacred relationships at the core of our lives, those with family, friends, and like-minded peers. Thus, we begin to climb up the mountain together and begin to see through our spiritual eyes and discern meaning in what we see.

Spiritual paths necessarily come with spiritual practices that need to be integrated into daily life. During these days of pandemic social distancing, David and I exchange Light most days and everyone in our family makes an effort to give and receive Light to the main soul daily. Mira, Ives, and David join me for weekly center service for the holy objects at the Pasadena Center, Rudy is starting to and Santanov hopes to do the same soon. I offer service at the center each week and we often clean the center when we're there. This is a special arrangement to purify and bring more Light into our souls and spiritual bodies and, through ourselves, into the world. This week I was inspired to clean the counters in the main hall. I have learned to connect with material blessings so much more deeply and gratefully through this practice and realize there is divine essence and sacred arrangement in everything in our world, animate and inanimate. We can receive and review spiritual development courses and offer special services like overnight center security or all-day Light giving. Every such step brings with it opportunities for purification with divine protection through Light giving, elevation, and divine arrangements for spiritual development. We also study divine books that fill us with divine energy. Part of my practice is reading the Goseigen regularly.

Our commitment, discipline, patience, and pure love grow as do our characteristic virtues. We grow to naturally influence and welcome connected souls to climb the mountain with us so Light, inspiration, and spiritual attunement in the world grows. We hope leaders and scientists will awaken to the importance of spirit and live daily lives in tune with divine will and principles. We pray that we will all help create the conditions in the world for divine wisdom to link with human wisdom, for elevated lives and minds to pave the way for elevated science. We hope it becomes possible for educational fields and institutions founded on external, impersonal, physical, human knowledge to be founded on divine wisdom, internal, personal, spiritual knowledge combined with human knowledge, knowing that spirit is first and the material follows. Our commitment to taking the U-turn in daily life holds the key to manifesting the divine principle of spirit first, mind next, body follows. In this work, every story is significant and the efforts of every true spiritual practitioner with their family, friends, and like-minded peers is sacred.

The stories you have read so far of the efforts of earlier generations, Roger and David, myself and my sister Shouma, and in the next generation of Santanov, Rudy, Ives, and Mira are efforts at varying levels of making this U-turn. They contain experiences of purification, elevation, and love. They reflect the divine love that allows the purifications and elevations, along with the love of Sukyo Mahikari staff members, fellow practitioners at centers, and family members whose Light giving and guidance give nourishment and support, as well as our own efforts to grow spiritually. These efforts are permitted by grace and powered by our own wills with the hope that the path of true happiness shines in homes and hearths throughout this world over a long course. It is an effort also powered by love to climb as one humanity to the summit of the mountain to see and treasure the world and all of nature through our spiritual eyes. Can we imagine this together?

Chapter 3

Spotlights

Mira Ambika Banerjee Brown

This chapter speaks to the understanding that our families are our first training in the practice of character and virtue. It's through our relationships with those closest to us that we come to know and see ourselves in our truest forms. I've come to understand that, for most of us, becoming a person who can give wholeheartedly and without attachment to others is a conscious undertaking. Before we can truly serve our communities on a larger scale, we have to become people who can see beyond ourselves as individuals, who understand the meaning of interdependence, and who are actually willing to make the sacrifices necessary to bring about real change. We are given the opportunity to not only train ourselves in these ways through family life, but to pass along the wisdom gained to generations to come. This book shows how spiritual practice makes this possible, not just for monastics and sages, but for us all.

Xiye Bastida

As the mother of four children and a giver of Light, Leena Banerjee Brown has been able to fulfill the vision of a spirit-centered family rooted in loving care that can be a living example of the foundations of a spiritually-grounded society. Her prayer that youth will cultivate the same elevation of mind that they wish for the planet is also my prayer. Many of us are cultivating mindfulness or some spiritual practice that brings us closer to Earth and this is clearing our minds and helping make U-turns in our everyday lives and in the structures that we are part of.

Pooja Verma

In these words lie a gentle call to action, the call to harmonize. Harmonizing happens in an active state, one in which we create things that are much greater than our individual whims and wants, one in which we face adversity and surprisingly turn it into opportunity, and one in which the self expands beyond perceived limitations. A hope is felt for this harmonious world in Leena's beautiful stories about her four bright and inspired children. Their experiences highlight how tapping into one's deeper intelligence, the intelligence that is aligned with your highest self, can lead to growth and the unification of disparate parts, whether those parts be factioned pieces of yourself or factioned groups. Spirituality and the tools to practice it nurture this highest self and turn compulsion and conflict into coherence and connectivity within the sacred family units we build and between generations today and generations to come. These pages lovingly invite us to climb up the mountain together and feel this powerful force that is both beyond us and aligned with something deep inside

of us. Although at times unbeknownst to us, this journey is also full of grace, as it quietly connects the dots that shape our futures into forms that make our eyes light up.

Chapter 4

Human-Nature Harmony

*T*he elevation of the mind through service to God is something I have personally experienced, witnessed through conscientious Light givers like Roger Beck, and hope to further cultivate in myself and in the world. Whether we are addressing environmental degradation, agricultural exploitation, or the myriad health and well-being issues facing humanity today, it is of great significance for scientists advancing any field to be of elevated mind if we are to protect our planet and create a world where all can thrive. This is equally true not only for scientists, but for all human beings.

I'm honored to share my stories as well as those of several friends who have experienced elevation of the mind through service to God. My personal experience records the evolution of my mental attitude of pure love for the earth, gardening, and parenting, through my relationships and activities with them. I began with a positive mind. Once I added the practice of True Light and universal principles to my actions, what evolved was a manifestation of spiritual elevation. Roger Beck's experience with and commitment to healthy eating and elevated consciousness regarding farming and food is like a beacon of hope as we face the realities and consequences of factory farming and other tragically flawed systems currently degrading God's creation. Some additional stories from several friends and acquaintances complement Roger's and my experiences, recognizing the reality that all people have been given opportunities to witness how harmony manifests in the world around us when we harmonize our spirit, mind, and body with God. I'm sure each of you currently reading this book could contribute stories of your own to this chapter.

It Begins in the Garden

In 1990, when Rudy and I moved to Pasadena, half-way across the world from my family in India, I began teaching psychology at the California School of Professional Psychology (which later became Alliant International University.) Rudy began attending a Montessori school. About six months later, I bought a condominium that had a large covered patio. I was drawn to this space, motivated by a strong desire to give of myself to the earth by growing a garden. I began spending time in the garden regularly, augmenting the flower bed by adding a number of pots. Before long, my efforts yielded a lovely, green, flourishing patio garden.

On Rudy's fifth birthday I bought him an orange tree, which we planted together in a large pot. Years later, when Ives and Mira came along, we repeated this tree planting tradition on each of their fifth birthdays. These traditions may not seem like a big deal, but the importance of honoring our children's connection with nature cannot be overstated. I recently heard the story of a father's emotional response to seeing his eleven-year-old son holding the very first apple he had harvested from a tree the boy had planted from a seed when he was three years old. This poignant moment spoke to me of the wisdom of staying connected to the earth with love, patience, and gratitude. It was moving to see that this was indeed being passed down from father to son.

Gardening—my small tribute to the earth—gave my young family such a large return: a place to tune in with nature without leaving home. Over time, my passion to expand my garden and my connection with the earth grew. I wanted to put my hands in the soil and grow life in it with my young son Rudy learning alongside me. Raising Rudy as a single parent, I was blessed to make a new friend at this time—a remarkable eighty-three-year-old woman—whose friendship with me continued to grow until she passed away at age ninety-three. She had a good-sized ranch of orange and lemon groves, located about twenty minutes from our home. I visited her regularly. One day, as I was telling her of my patio garden and my deep wish to garden with my son, she pointed to a sunny spot on the ranch right outside her home and said "Take that piece of land, Leena, grow whatever you wish on it." Grateful beyond words, we began to put our hands in the soil to grow tomatoes, cucumbers, and zucchini. This garden had the richest, most fertile, healthy soil you could imagine, and it received lots of sun. We had bountiful harvests, which we shared with friends and still had more than we could eat.

Fast forward a few years to our present home where David and I have raised Rudy, Ives, and Mira, and where Santanov lived with us for two years. Here, we ourselves have some space where we put our hands in the soil to grow things. The gift of this connection with the earth overwhelmed me with so much gratitude that I dedicated my Sunday mornings for many years to working in our garden. From time to time the children and I gardened together, sometimes David joined in, and when my mother visited us from India, she put her hands in. Her planting of a little bayleaf tree has grown as tall as a cedar, and several other succulents are also thriving. In those days, my father was there too, and I remember well, with appreciation, each of his suggestions to add splashes of color in the garden.

This commitment to gardening with my family came from deep inside me. Slowly, I got to know every part of the garden. All the plants in the garden found their right places and flourished. This made the mother in me smile. I realized that when our motivations are pure, our actions are filled with the vibrations of altruistic, selfless love. They come into alignment with God, and thus become our divine prayer. When we act in this way, our actions naturally produce fulfillment and joy. I experienced this in the garden with my family in a way that was foundational to my spiritual development. For me, it was a precursor of sorts to the spiritual life I would later embrace.

When I was introduced to the art of True Light and took the primary spiritual development course, I glimpsed a fundamental truth: great love permeates the universe, manifesting in universal principles and laws of arrangement. I learned that all material existence is composed of elementary particles, which arise from the invisible realm through the laws of arrangement established by God. When our innermost consciousness is truly in harmony with God, we may be allowed to materialize parts of material existence. Spirit is first, mind next, and the physical follows, as you will see in this next story.

One of my most profound experiences of true harmony occurred in the garden. There is a corner in our sunny Southern California backyard where a little shade was wanted. "I wish we could have a little shade in this sunny corner," I would say aloud to myself—shade that does not interfere with the open sky in the rest of the backyard. We tried different human-made methods of creating shade such as a garden umbrella and a carport, but these structures proved unsatisfactory in the long run. Eventually, we gave up. The wish for shade in the corner of the garden retreated to the recesses of my mind.

I gave True Light to the garden almost every day, purifying its spiritual core and essence. As I gave True Light, I often offered prayers for the preservation and restoration of the whole earth and the interconnected web of life it holds. A couple of years later, I was weeding around the patio area in the corner in which we wanted shade. I noticed three sturdy weeds. I tried to uproot them and could not. I asked David to try and he could not. We asked our gardener to try and he could not. We were surprised by these hardy weeds' refusal to be evicted from our yard. We decided to just leave them alone and promptly forgot about them.

A few months later, we noticed them again—and this time we realized they were not weeds. They were trees! They were Chinese elms that grow easily in Los Angeles soil with very little water. They are actually protected trees in this area, and they were placed by unseen hands exactly where we wanted shade. When we realized they were a gift from God we celebrated their arrival. They continue to thrive as beautiful shade-giving trees with round canopies, symmetrical leaves, and drooping branches that embrace you as you sit in their shade. They have created a most natural, beautiful, peaceful corner of shade in our garden. A far greater variety of birds make our backyard their home because of them, especially these days as wildfires rage throughout this area and much of the western coast of the North American continent, displacing birds from their habitat. I see new birds flitting in and out of the trees in our garden enveloped in a smoky haze. The other day I saw a sole golden oriole for the first time! I am filled with wonder, gratitude, and humility that they perch in these trees which materialized in such a mysterious way. Ideal, beautiful trees, ideally placed.

I am still incredulous at the appearance of these trees in our garden, and I marvel at them almost every time I see them. Their arrival is a mystery beyond my human ability to grasp. I do understand, though, that this little miracle reflects the principle of true harmony—harmony in the three dimensions of spirit, mind, and body. Harmony that was facilitated simply through giving True Light with a pure innermost attitude and elevated mind. I was seeking to connect with the divine and to serve as an instrument of God's will by radiating True Light—penetrating the interconnected, unseen, and seen realms of spirit, mind, and body as they manifest in heaven, sky, and earth. Just as Rabindranath Tagore may have been divinely guided to create his school at

Santiniketan under the canopy of trees, these divinely planted trees have begun a transformation process in our yard, which is now on its way to becoming a serene sanctuary for those whose hearts of divine service seek Light, for it is where our holy Goshintai room will soon be built. I feel grounded and free here, just as I did during my childhood summers at Santiniketan. Working in my garden in Pasadena, offering True Light each day, I am allowed to participate in its elevation to a sacred place—a place in which others may also find the path to be grounded and free through divine connection, divine service, and self transformation.

Before integrating spirituality in my daily life, such an experience was beyond imagining for me. Daily spiritual practice involving the unseen realm, developing my mind's capacity for reflection and elevation, and getting in touch with my true self were all contributing steps toward making the wondrous and extraordinary possible and visible in my life. I now see how deeply we are connected with nature, and with all that is around us—and thus how deep our responsibility is to care for it all—not only for ourselves, but also for posterity. It reminds me of the truth reflected in Michelangelo's painting "The Creation of Adam" in which God extends a hand down to touch humankind's. I see the painting as an artistic expression of the principle of spirit, mind, and body that I experienced in the garden.

My garden experience also showed me that any of us ordinary human beings can bring ourselves into alignment with God if we are willing to integrate spirituality in our daily lives. We each have the potential to contribute to the materialization of a beautiful and peaceful world. It actually is possible.

I nurture my family's spiritual development and stewardship of the earth through my steadfast daily presence and spiritual practice, and through embracing the members of my family in theirs. The deep environmentalism and humanitarianism of their work and daily life reflect the divine guidance we receive, as well as the efforts we make together. When I see how the next generation is taking this commitment to the next level, I anticipate the advancement of science through elevated, integrated minds that make sense of subjective experience and objective information and strive to harmonize with divine wisdom.

Roger Beck's Garden as a Window on Nature

"God created nature as an interdependent web of life in which all life forms can flourish," Roger Beck stated with a satisfied grin on his serene face. He knows firsthand that agriculture and food production are indeed part of nature, not only to sustain human life, but in making us a beneficiary of nature in a very primal way. Sustaining human life in the long run requires an environment in which nature is healthy and prospering.

Roger recognizes humanity as the highest life form, and he asserts that we have a responsibility to protect and support nature. Because we have been assigned the role of supporting life on earth—a sacred responsibility—God has equipped us with exceptional minds, diverse physical abilities, and the divine spark necessary to do the job well. But, Roger laments, our material-first civilization has often exploited nature in the name of the endless pursuit of material benefits for individuals, businesses, and/or society. As we all know, the resulting environmental damage has been catastrophic. But Roger's approach to harmonizing with the environment, which was initially linked to his efforts to overcome rheumatoid arthritis, is as inspirational as it is instructional.

As a professor of economics, Roger has been studying and teaching about the human use of resources for many years. He traces exploitation of the natural world back to the fifteenth century, giving the example of how competition among tribes on Easter Island as they built stone statues led to the complete extinction of the largest variety of palm tree ever discovered. Those big-headed statues were too heavy to lift, so palm trees were used as rollers to skid statues from the quarry to the tribe's land.[8] The residents of Easter Island may have intended to honor their ancestors by erecting statues, but they did not know how to honor God by respecting nature. Clearly, elimination of this unique palm tree variety clashes with the universal principle of treating materials preciously and supporting life on earth.

As in the Easter Island case, one type of over-exploitation of nature Roger often taught his classes is known as "the tragedy of the commons." This rather dramatic name was coined in the late 1960s to describe the situation that arises when property rights over a resource are not defined—meaning no one entity has ownership and the right to exclude others. In such cases, all nations, businesses, or persons who want to use the resource have an incentive to hurry to use it before a competitor does. A valuable resource in which there is no property right or effective regulatory control will be over-exploited, and possibly used up entirely. Ocean fisheries are a conspicuous example. The cod fishery off the eastern coast of Canada no longer exists because of exactly this problem. Government regulation was ineffective in restraining competitive fishing, resulting in the total exhaustion of the cod fishery.

There are many different commons, including the air we breathe, forests on public land, and the water in our lakes and rivers. Without a property right, it is difficult to effectively limit pollution of the commons. It is true that some control is exercised over some of these commons through regulation by government. However, it has not been possible to prove that regulation by any government has provided any commons with optimal protection against pollution. In fact, there is reason to believe that government itself often is a major polluter, and also that government sometimes aids and abets pollution by business. Perhaps spiritual development will trump government as an impetus to change the way we manage resources to a more caring model.[9]

Roger taught the problem of the commons in his undergraduate and graduate economics classes throughout his career, but it was later in his life that he himself began to see its greater spiritual implications. "I've been on a personal learning curve with respect to the environment, as has our society," Roger confesses. Around 1970, he attended a debate at the University of Chicago between one of his professors and another economist. His professor (who later received a Nobel Prize in economics) stoutly asserted that environmentalism was a fad that would quickly fade away. To the contrary, however, both awareness of environmental issues and initiatives to curtail environmental degradation have greatly expanded since 1970. Roger now recognizes that this expansion aligns with the universal principle to treat resources preciously—as a manifestation of our gratitude to their Creator in ways that are consistent with the responsibility of humankind to support nature.

Roger's knowledge of environmental issues initially arose from what he saw as his responsibilities as a member of society, giving him a degree of detachment. Environmental issues became more personal when Roger realized that his health had been affected by environmental toxins, as he has shared in the story surrounding his rheumatoid arthritis. In his early efforts to address his symptoms, Roger recognized that careful choices with regard to his diet would be very important to his well-being. But it was following Sukyo Mahikari spiritual practices that caused his symptoms of rheumatoid arthritis to disappear entirely. Roger's arthritis was replaced by a feeling of very deep gratitude toward God. He expressed his gratitude by undertaking Sukyo Mahikari spiritual practices with gradually increasing intensity, which in turn, has gradually increased Roger's commitment to nature.

Roger actually credits his rheumatoid arthritis with inspiring him to integrate spirituality into his daily life. "What great blessings my arthritis brought me!" Roger now says with an incredulous smile. He had been free of arthritic symptoms for more than twenty years when they gradually began to reappear. This time, rather than placing his primary focus on getting rid of his symptoms, Roger's goal was to learn the new lessons God was leading him to master. By expectantly looking for the deeper personal message and spiritual meaning being offered to him through divine wisdom, Roger's arthritis has been transformed from what he initially feared was a curse to the blessing he now accepts it as. Thus, Sukyo Mahikari spiritual practices have given him a path of life-long learning in harmony with God.

Reflecting on this, Roger told me "Some time ago, I had the spiritual realization that there really are no accidents, in the sense that everything occurs for a good reason. I understand the circumstances of my life unfold over time in a way God arranges to encourage my spiritual growth." This includes everything we learn through study and day-to-day experience. Thus, changes in circumstances provide opportunities to practice gratitude, acceptance, and humility--the three great virtues we cultivate to help us harmonize with other universal principles.

Once he befriended his arthritis as the blessing of purification it came to be, Roger was led to a key person who could help him better understand its underlying causes. A friend of his who was struggling with cancer told him that, after consulting with thirty different doctors, he had finally found one who could help him overcome his cancer—Dr. Stephen Genuis, M.D. (Yes, it is fitting that his name is very close to the word "genius!") Intrigued by his friend's description of this doctor's methods, Roger decided to consult with him. Dr. Genuis practices scientific medicine, but with greater insight than any doctor Roger had ever met. Dr. Genuis embraces the view that every illness has a cause, and so, the goal of modern medicine should be to find the cause and eliminate it. Consistent with his focus on scientific medicine, he is a prolific researcher of medical questions, and most of his many papers are available online.[10] Pointing out that the Latin root of the word "doctor" means teacher, Dr. Genuis is committed to educating his patients about cause and effect. He gives a lecture each week to his patients, recording it for those who cannot attend. Roger recognizes the value of this approach, but what he appreciates most about Dr. Genuis is his humility. Roger recognizes that Dr. Genuis' practice of medicine is on a very high level spiritually, which may explain his extraordinary ability to guide his patients back to health.

After listening to one of Dr. Genuis' lectures as a guest of his friend, Roger applied to become a patient. About ten months later, he had moved to the top of the waiting list and began consulting with Dr. Genuis. His first step was to complete an eighty-page questionnaire, yielding the most complete history Roger had ever provided to any doctor. Roger was impressed at his next visit that Dr. Genuis had clearly read this "magnum opus" closely, bringing his own hand-written notes to his appointment with Roger.

Each month Dr. Genuis introduced a new step in the protocol, which struck Roger as being consistent with the universal principle of "step-by-step" applicable in undertaking any kind of major change (such as integrating spirituality in daily life). A step-by-step approach helps to ensure the patient is not overwhelmed or discouraged by the magnitude of the challenge in recovering health. At the outset, patients undergo very thorough laboratory analysis of blood and urine samples, after following procedures designed to flush some toxins out of body tissues and into these fluids. In addition to identification of the body's toxin levels, the tests also measure levels of key nutrients and assess the effectiveness of some of the body's metabolic processes.

These tests—not covered by the Canadian health care system—are expensive. Roger's retirement income is limited, but God provided the resources he needed when he needed them, for which he expresses immense gratitude. Roger's tests indicated extremely high levels of three heavy metals (aluminum, cadmium, and arsenic), as well as high levels of pesticides and other toxins present in Roger's body. And so, Roger's awareness that dietary and environmental factors were relevant to his arthritis were confirmed and his commitment to organic living increased.

Dr. Genuis explained to Roger that as the body is exposed to more and more toxins, a point is reached where the immune system can no longer function normally. The immune system begins to attack the body itself—for example, the cartilage in the joints. Thus, rheumatoid arthritis manifests. The solution is to help the body eliminate toxins, to avoid further toxic exposure, and to ensure the body has all the nutrients it needs for repair. As toxin levels drop and nutrition improves, eventually the immune system resumes normal functioning and symptoms disappear.

Interestingly, Dr. Genuis' explanation of arthritis is consistent with a plausible explanation for the initial disappearance of Roger's arthritic symptoms at the time he began giving and receiving True Light. Giving and receiving True Light is a process of purification, a process that would include the elimination of toxins. So, Roger's arthritic symptoms may have disappeared because True Light melted and eliminated an accumulation of toxins. Arthritic symptoms may have returned because Roger accumulated toxins more rapidly than he eliminated them through giving and receiving True Light. In addition to physical/environmental, mental/emotional toxins there are spiritual toxins that can relate to previous lives and those of ancestors, the purification of which are divine blessings relating to spiritual elevation of the vibration of innermost attitude and true harmony with God.

For a number of years, there were no other True Light practitioners in the area where Roger lives. Consequently, he did not receive True Light from others or give to them daily as often as he had in previous years (which typically has more impact than giving True Light to oneself, as this cultivates the spirit of selfless giving and attunement with God). But thankfully, Dr. Genuis' intervention for Roger was complementary to giving and receiving True Light. When we experience cleansing or purification in the form of a health issue, True Light practitioners are encouraged to combine Sukyo Mahikari spiritual practices with medical science. Some of the toxins accumulated in Roger's body may have come from exposure to environmental toxins, from mental or emotional sources, from his ancestors, from all humankind, or from some combination of these sources. These impurities are unlikely to be removed through medical science alone. When we experience a health issue, we are being given an opportunity to improve our innermost attitude through coming to grips with our impurities. A combination of medical science and spiritual practice is then applied.

Another possible explanation for Roger's returning arthritis is failure to learn some important spiritual lesson. Roger has shared, in deep humility, that his character is such that, minute-by-minute, he tends to be active in the pursuit of a particular goal. Yet often the outcome falls short of his goal. And so, lingering feelings of dissatisfaction and complaint that accompany this high-achiever mentality may create toxins of their own. As Roger considered this possibility, he realized that feelings of dissatisfaction and complaint would also reflect a demanding attitude toward God—which suggests insufficient gratitude for God's many blessings. Such feelings of dissatisfaction and complaint (if we have them) would likely create toxins in our body. On the other hand, gratitude for perceiving these inner negativities and apology for them gives momentum to the effort to elevate our innermost attitude and harmonize with God in the process of spiritual development. By improving our practice of gratitude for the outcomes actually achieved and becoming more accepting of the results flowing from our best efforts, we might reduce or eliminate the causes of our cleansing. Although Dr. Genuis' approach doesn't acknowledge the spiritual realm, its goals of purification complement the spiritual goals taught in Sukyo Mahikari.

But material goals never produce the spiritual gifts we truly crave. By achieving a better balance between material goals and spiritual goals, we also balance our pursuit of personal benefit with service to others. If we think of ourselves as striving to achieve true health through constant efforts to regain and maintain the physical abilities God intends humankind to have, it's best to bear in mind that the purpose of better health is to more effectively serve God, lest we become excessively self-absorbed in pursuit of true health.

As Roger explored possible explanations for his returning arthritis, whether it was caused by shortfalls in practicing universal principles or exposure to environmental toxins or a combination thereof, I was struck by the absence of self-judgment or self-criticism in Roger's demeanor, even as he acknowledged his need for personal change. Roger's pure desire to learn what God was teaching him in this recurrence of arthritis modeled for me how to use my mind's deep reflective capacity to probe for new meaning in my daily experiences, most powerfully during visits to my Sukyo Mahikari center. The center is a beacon of hope where we harmonize with God by elevating our innermost attitude. Such possibility brings with it hope for change in our physical condition, as we come to know that spirit is first, mind next, and body follows.

Roger's partnership with Dr. Genuis was arranged by God not only to help him overcome the effects of rheumatoid arthritis in his own body, but to increase his knowledge about the effects of environmental toxins on the planet and all of its residents. Roger's knowledge of the pervasive distribution of toxins vastly increased as a result of office visits with Dr. Genuis and listening to his lectures. Roger is both shocked and appalled at the widespread distribution of environmental toxins, about which many people may be somewhat aware, but most people have no idea of the vast extent of this very serious problem.

Roger's understanding of the spiritual dimension of the environmental toxin problem is that it is extremely urgent, spiritually, for humankind to make strenuous efforts to return the earth to its original pure condition. This purpose is consistent with our responsibilities as caretakers of the earth and supporters of nature. It is also consistent with the need to ensure that nature is sufficiently free of toxins to support life, including human life, in the long run.

Indeed, our food supply has become badly contaminated, causing diseases that are so widespread we've just come to accept them as inevitable. Although there is a huge amount of evidence to show that toxins are nearly everywhere—found in umbilical cord blood of newborns, in rainwater, and in the soil itself—and that our health is failing as a result, it's clear we are not doing enough to stem the flow of toxins into our environment. Roger has taken this call to action very seriously, as you will see in his commitment to restoring healthy farming practices and promoting a radically changed approach to food production.

Prior to his introduction to Sukyo Mahikari in 1986, recall that Roger had been searching for a way to recover from rheumatoid arthritis beginning in 1979. As he searched for the causes of his deteriorating health, one of the possibilities he examined was food. Having never paid much attention to any connection between food and health prior to his diagnosis, Roger learned that impurities (pesticides, herbicides, chemical fertilizers, etc.) in food may be linked to autoimmune dysfunction.

Of course, we all want to avoid impurities. But even when free of impurities, some foods might have components that aggravate arthritis. For example, many people believe the nightshade family of vegetables worsens arthritis by increasing inflammation. Roger discovered arguments in favor of a variety of different diets, such as a high-alkaline diet, a macrobiotic diet, a non-red-meat diet, a vegetarian diet, etc. But, looking back now, he can see that God was making arrangements to raise his consciousness. Food was the subject, and is indeed a very important part of life, but what I witnessed in Roger was a spiritual approach to this very physical issue.

In the Sukyo Mahikari primary spiritual development course, we learn there is no restrictive subset of available foods that is the right diet for all humankind. The body was designed to send signals to the brain enabling choice of the right foods to meet the body's needs. But Roger points out that what we learn in the primary spiritual development course often is not really accepted as our own truth until we have our own personal experiences confirming what we were told. And so, Roger continued his quest for a specific diet designed to cure his rheumatoid arthritis.

While researching the impact of food choices on health, Roger was led to the work of a dentist named Weston A. Price. Dr. Price visited what he called "primitive" people in remote places around the world during the first half of the twentieth century to examine their diets in relation to their dental health, as well as their general physical health. The evidence he collected showed that traditional diets were the key to dental health, and he found a connection between the state of dental health and the health of the whole body. He showed that when people switch from indigenous to modern diets, both dental health and general health quickly deteriorate.

Dr. Price's work also suggests that avoiding modern processed foods is not only essential for optimal health but is also essential in order for people to be of good character. This caused Roger to wonder if there may be a relationship between modern food and failure of citizens in modern societies to live in accordance with universal principles. For example, people often fail to treat each other with altruistic love, hold themselves to ethical standards which may be beyond legal ones, develop conscience, character, and wisdom. Indigenous peoples tend to be deeply grateful as they eat, feeling their connection with nature and its life-sustaining bounty. "Could it be," Roger asked, "that modern foods retard the progress of those seeking to develop themselves spiritually?" Interestingly, Dr. Price found that the diets of indigenous peoples varied widely, consistent with the tenet that there is no subset of available foods that is a required diet for all humankind.

But the source of the food we eat is of utmost importance. In Roger's personal study, he traced farming back to about 10,000 BCE, when crops started to replace hunting/gathering as humans' source of food. Roger found no evidence from Price's early twentieth-century investigations of indigenous groups to suggest that traditional farming practices undermined health. The same cannot be said for farming in modern societies, where adverse health effects are well documented. Choosing methods to maximize profits without adequately considering the effects of those methods on food quality and on consumers probably has been an important driver leading to adverse health effects. Also, the mindset of relationship, interconnectedness, and stewardship is not as common in farming in modern societies as it was historically, and probably quite rare in food processing.

Yoko Farming

As Roger continued to change on a deep level by integrating spirituality into his daily life, his approach to food changed from a physically-oriented one to a spiritually-oriented one. God arranged for him to learn about an agricultural method Sukyo Mahikari calls yoko farming. Right away, yoko farming became an extension of his efforts to improve and maintain his physical and spiritual health, as well as to share spiritually high-level foods with others. Roger learned that Sukyo Mahikari had established the first yoko farm, the Nyukawa Yoko Farm, on five acres near Takayama, Japan in 1985. Since then, yoko farms have been established in many countries throughout the world.

Yoko farming is most simply defined as organic farming with the application of True Light and universal principles. The four central purposes of yoko farming are as follows:

1. To facilitate the spiritual elevation of all those involved—farmers, consumers, and purveyors, allowing all involved to come closer to God through contact with nature.

2. To produce food that is highly nutritious due to both physical content and high-level spiritual vibrations—able to more powerfully support human life and health.

3. To be not just sustainable, but restorative of the soil's original pure condition.

4. To continually elevate the spiritual aspect of the physical farm itself, as well as its farm products.

Profit is not a primary goal of yoko farming. Rather, the farmer and the farm are in service to God, humankind, and nature.

To better understand what is meant in by "high-level spiritual vibrations" in farm products, Roger observed an experiment carried out at the Nyukawa Yoko Farm as part of a day's education for a group of yoko farming trainees. The group gathered at the end of a plastic hoop greenhouse, where the instructor asked for a volunteer in his demonstration. A young man from Australia came forward. The instructor harvested a cucumber from the vines growing in the hoop house and handed it to the Australian, who held it in his right hand. The Australian was asked to extend his left arm parallel to the ground. The instructor pushed down on his arm, telling the Australian to resist the pressure, and he was able to keep his extended arm parallel to the ground. Next, the instructor asked the Australian to step on the cucumber. Reluctantly, he did so—not squashing the cucumber, but damaging it. Then, as he again held the cucumber in his right hand and extended his left arm, the instructor easily pushed his left arm down to his side. Finally, the instructor asked the Australian to apologize to the cucumber. After apologizing, and again extending his left arm parallel to the ground, the instructor could not push the Australian's left arm down.

Roger inferred from this experiment that there are spiritual vibrations in vegetables and in our attitudes and actions, and these vibrations vary as to level.

Initially, the cucumber's spiritual vibrations were high, as was the Australian's attitude toward it, as reflected in the added strength in the Australian's left arm while he was holding the cucumber in his right hand. After stepping on the cucumber, the person and the vegetable's spiritual vibrations plummeted, and the Australian's arm strength was diminished. Lastly, the vibration of an apology from the Australian mysteriously restored a higher level of spiritual vibrations in him and the cucumber, as shown by the instructor's inability to make the Australian's left arm yield to a downward push. The existence of these spiritual vibrations implies that the manner in which farm products are treated will have a significant effect on their spiritual vibrations, and thus on the spiritual vibrations contained in the food we place on our tables.

I'm reminded of the Jewish tradition of Shabbat where three blessings take place as the sabbath begins each Friday evening: first the blessing of the candles, then of wine or juice, and then of a sweet leavened bread called challah. The bread is initially covered with a cloth, which might seem like a wise thing to do to keep it fresh or keep flies off it. But actually, the cloth is there so the bread won't be insulted to see that it is the last item to be blessed. When the time for the bread's blessing arrives, the cloth is removed and everyone present gasps in admiration of the bread's beauty. The message to all participating in Shabbat is that if we should take such care about the feelings of a loaf of bread, we should also take care of the feelings of all people and all of creation.

Many of us buy vegetables in our grocery store that have been raised thousands of miles away and handled by many people before we buy them. Beef, chicken, and pork sold in grocery stores often come from animals that have been crowded together in feedlots, or densely populated chicken factories and pig farms. It is plausible that the spiritual vibrations of these grocery store foods have been lowered by the manner in which the animals and vegetables were treated. Perhaps after we buy them we should begin by apologizing to our food for any mistreatment at the hands of farmers, shippers, or retailers. Sukyo

Mahikari members are advised to give True Light to their food, and that would certainly be a helpful complement to a vibration of apology.

Roger shares a personal experience to explain why the level of spiritual vibrations in our food matters. His metabolism is such that he has always consumed large quantities of food, taking second helpings as a matter of course, often followed by third helpings. One day he was part of a group having lunch in a Sukyo Mahikari cafeteria in Japan where all the vegetables came from the Nyukawa Yoko Farm. Roger passed through the cafeteria line and filled his plate. He found the food extraordinarily tasty, so having finished his first helping, he passed through the cafeteria line again for a second helping. But when he began eating his second helping, he realized he was no longer hungry. Roger concluded that the spiritual vibrations as well as the nutritional content of the yoko farm food were so high that a single helping was all that was needed to satisfy his hearty appetite. Roger asserts that it is a reasonable conjecture that, on average per unit of food, yoko farm food makes a larger contribution to sustaining our lives and health.

When asked what makes a yoko farm different, Roger shared that in addition to following organic farming practices, farmers on yoko farms give True Light to seeds, plants (including weeds), soil (with awareness of the crucial role of soil microbes), animals, insects, farm equipment, tools, and harvested food. Yoko farmers aim to speak only words that project positive vibrations, and train themselves with the goal to have only positive thoughts when farming. Weeds and all insects are seen to have an important role to play in nature, and their role is respected and accepted. For example, both weeds and insects may have the role to improve the quality of the soil. There are times, however, when weeds and insects have completed their work.

Yoko farmers also endeavor to think and act in ways that reflect love and gratitude for all aspects of nature. Roger gets very excited when telling about the positive environmental impact of yoko farming. He feels that the spread of Yoko farming has the potential to make a major contribution toward overcoming the damage to farmland and people resulting from conventional farming practices. He loves to speak of the many amazing results that come from practicing yoko farming. For example, in the Fukushima area of Japan—the site of the tsunami-caused nuclear power plant accident in 2011—produce from a yoko farmer's fields had no detectable radiation contamination. Measurements from neighboring farmers' fields, however, showed significant radiation contamination.[11]

Roger trained at the Nyukawa Yoko Farm for a few days at a time over several years beginning in the late 1990s. After he retired from the University of Alberta, he established a small yoko farm in the mountains of British Columbia. In addition to enjoying the multiple benefits of yoko farming himself, he was thrilled to be able to share yoko farm vegetables with friends and neighbors. For about ten years, he sold vegetables and sauerkraut, and was delighted to hear from many who bought his produce that they had never before had such tasty food on their dining tables. Of course, these vegetables were filled with True Light! Roger always marvels at the high quality of the vegetables he eats, grown on his yoko farm, compared to vegetables he eats elsewhere. Occasionally, he buys organic vegetables at a health food store or farmers' market, but these also are less appealing than his yoko farm vegetables.

Roger even loves the insects that many other farmers consider pests. The premise that insects have a valuable role to play in improving the quality of the soil suggests that insects attack plants when the quality of the soil is inadequate to sustain healthy plants. Some think of the unhealthy plants as inviting the insects to attack them in order to return plant parts to the soil, thus adding to its nutritional base. In Roger's yoko farm, he has seen behavior consistent with this way of thinking. He had two adjacent rows of carrots planted at two different times. The early batch of carrots was in soil that he knew to be of lower quality. When these carrots matured, slugs immediately attacked them.

His first thought was not about the lower quality of the soil, but instead, Roger made a mental note to harvest the other row of carrots as soon as they matured to prevent any damage by slugs. However, when the second row of carrots matured, there was no sign of slugs. That's when he realized what he had observed supported the idea that insects usually attack weak plants growing in lower quality soil. The primary crop used to improve the quality of the soil on Roger's yoko farm is called "green manure." Different types of seeds can be used for this purpose, some of which (like field peas) fix nitrogen in the soil.

There are a number of inferences to be drawn from Roger's description of yoko farming principles, practices, and experiences. If you want to optimize your health and the health of the planet, Roger suggests you obtain your food from a yoko farm. If you don't have a yoko farm nearby, he suggests you might consider becoming a yoko farmer. If neither option is possible, he suggests you buy food from local farmers, preferably organic farmers, and learn to give Light to your food, thus maximizing purity, freshness, and nutritional content while minimizing handling. Roger urges us all to learn as much as we can about our suppliers' farming practices and buy from those in whom you have the greatest confidence.

When I first came to North America in 1981, I had a deeply meaningful experience with food, which I later realized was spiritual, though inchoate, in that I could not fully articulate it then. The first grocery store I entered was in Blacksburg, Virginia. I was astonished by the huge amount of food I saw—far more than I had ever seen at a store in India. My eyes filled with tears as I thought of my family in India who did not have access to this much food. There was something deeper than this as well, a grief for the human family that I now realize as I reflect on the thought that arose in my mind then: "All this food is dead. It has no life in it at all. I am not drawn to it at all." As I tasted grocery store food, I found that although food is plentiful in the United States, the taste is less flavorful and completely different from the less plentiful but flavorful, largely organic food I grew up with in the India of my childhood.

The practice of yoko farming produces such tasty food that is not only organic but is filled with Light and a commitment on the part of the farmer, distribution network, and consumer to grow spiritually in tune with nature restoring the soil on which we live. The appearance of research yoko farms in different parts of the world, committed to learning and spreading the practice of yoko farming will be a dream come true in materializing human-nature harmony.

Roger warns that although buying certified organic food protects against some toxins, it does not mean there are no toxins in the food. Here's an example Roger shared: certified organic brown rice in North America typically includes high levels of arsenic because rice in the southeastern United States is often grown on land formerly used to farm cotton with the help of arsenic, and rice from California may be grown with the help of chicken manure, and arsenic is often used in raising chickens. More generally, he warns that airborne pollution and waterborne pollution can contaminate certified organic food despite the commitment of organic farmers not to introduce those toxins in their farming.

Roger traces farming with chemical fertilizers back to the years following World War II. Chemical factories that had been built to produce explosives for waging war were converted to the production of fertilizer after the war. Chemical fertilizer degrades the soil and pollutes the environment, evidenced by the way runoff from American farm fields has resulted in a huge dead zone in the Gulf of Mexico devoid of key forms of ocean life. Pesticides and herbicides also pollute the environment, including groundwater. They leave toxic residues on vegetables, which accumulate in human bodies, causing illness.

Roger is especially concerned about the development of technology for genetic modification. Profit-seeking agricultural giants have genetically modified important crops to make them immune to the effects of a herbicide containing glyphosate used to kill "weeds." The producers of these genetically modified seeds preferred not to test whether genetically modified food is safe for human consumption even as animals fed genetically modified soybeans developed changes in internal organs—liver, pancreas, intestinal, and testicular tissue—compared to animals fed unmodified soybeans. When this herbicide was first introduced, the manufacturer claimed that glyphosate was non-toxic to humans and would not accumulate in the human body. Claims that have been proven erroneous and have been reinforced by the World Health Organization of the United Nations' recognition of glyphosate as a probable carcinogen in 2015.[12] And humans aren't the only ones suffering from the prevalence of chemical herbicides. Bees, which are pollinators essential to the production of much of our food, are being killed in high numbers by a newer class of herbicide, causing a significant reduction of our bee population.

Our Animal Partners

As you might imagine, farming practices that recognize the sacred qualities of plants and insects hold all living creatures in high esteem and treat them with loving apology for the ways humans disturb their environments. An extraordinary and very precious story shared by a Japanese tea farmer provides a contrasting experience to the factory farming approach. In the third year after shifting from conventional agriculture to yoko farming practices, the farmer went to the tea plantation one morning to find that many of the tea trees had been uprooted and destroyed by wild boars in the middle of the night. He thought to himself, "Due to environmental destruction brought about by human activity, the boars have little to eat. That's why they came to the fields last night." While apologizing to all of nature and its creatures, he gave True Light to the fields. The next morning when he went to the fields, he was shocked to see what lay before his eyes. During the night the boars had returned to the fields and used their tusks and snouts to spread organic compost on all of the raised beds—in the entire plantation of 9,900 square meters! It would have taken his entire family three whole days to do this work. Moreover, none of the tea trees were harmed! Amazingly, in the twenty-two years since then, the boars have come every year to help spread compost in the family fields. From this profound experience, the tea farmer deeply realized the importance of having an attitude of coexisting and co-prospering with nature.

Roger laments one of the most tragic byproducts of agricultural industrialization in terms of universal principles, that is, forcing many food animals to live their lives in an environment they were not designed to live in, and feeding some of them food they were not designed to eat. For example, God designed cattle to eat grass and live in pastures. Roger disagrees with the way factory farms feed them corn and confine them in feedlots, where drugs are essential to keep them nominally healthy. Similarly, chickens were intended to be free-range, but the predominant farming method today is to confine them in overcrowded cages. Factory farm pigs are so unsuited to the confines of their environment that it is common practice to amputate their tails because their stress levels are so high, they will otherwise bite each other's tails off. I agree with Roger's assessment of these horribly inhumane and spiritually devoid farming practices.

Roger argues that these agricultural practices clash with nature because our dominant farming practices are unsuited to the intrinsic nature of our food animals. He points out that it wouldn't be surprising if our mistreatment of these animal species caused vibrations of resentment toward humankind. In addition, he asserts that cattle farmed in feedlot filth and fed corn and drugs are not going to be healthy for us to eat, but they will be cheap to buy and profitable to farm. Spiritual practice and study of universal principles breaks down the material-first mentality at the root of this greed-based farming economy. This is an especially important realization for elevation in consciousness and practice during the COVID-19 pandemic, in which virus transfer has occurred from animals to humans. The spirit-first mentality of yoko farming has the capacity to transform the way humanity feeds itself and treats our fellow animal, insect, and plant life.

Outside the profit and greed motivated travesties of factory farming, we have many opportunities to harmonize with nature in the wild and in our everyday lives. May the following stories lift your spirits, dear reader, and heal the heartache that may have been caused by the previous section exposing the agricultural wrongs we must right by supporting yoko farming.

Dot Holland Lessard, who has taken both the primary and secondary Sukyo Mahikari spiritual development courses, tells a fascinating story of humans effectively communicating with wild animals. Since childhood, Dot has always felt a deep connection to the realm of nature, so she is thrilled to be blessed with a farm, an old apple orchard, and a large pond—all teeming with abundant wildlife. A few years ago, she heard a Sukyo Mahikari staff person speak of the importance of being in harmony with nature. He related how Sukyo Mahikari members in Japan are teaching local farmers to harmonize with nature when other creatures threaten their crops. In one case, rice farmers were losing crops to birds that ate the rice kernels. The farmers were shown how to explain to the birds that they should only eat what their mothers fed them as baby birds, in order to restore harmony and balance. Once it was explained to the birds that they should eat grubs, larvae, and other small insects, they stopped damaging the rice crops.

Interestingly, it was only a few days after Dot heard about the Japanese farmers that a beaver arrived at her family's farm. With plenty of trees nearby and deep water, the pond offered ideal homesteading conditions for this new visitor. Over the years several beavers had taken up residence in the pond, sometimes resulting in the loss of many trees and stopping the flow of water from the pond into the surrounding pastures. If ignored, this beaver would soon be busy taking down trees for a new dam, transforming the landscape in ways that weren't congruent with Dot's family's use of that space. In the past, Dot and her husband had had a difference of opinion about the best way to handle the problem. Fortunately, this time he was willing to accept Dot's approach to managing the situation—until the beaver takes down the first tree. After that, his more abrupt approach would be pursued.

Soon after noticing the beaver in the pond, Dot stood on the dock and offered a prayer, gave True Light to the surrounding area, then spoke aloud to the beaver. She respectfully explained that they would like him to leave the pond and that he would be in danger if he caused damage by taking down trees and blocking the flow of water. Dot explained to the beaver that the trees around the pond were important for filtering and maintaining clean water, further explaining that the water flowing from the pond crisscrossed the surrounding pastures, providing much needed water for grazing cattle and horses. She also wrote a note with the same information and placed it against a tree on the side of the pond where she had last seen the beaver. Of course she understood that beavers don't read, but by writing to them Dot communicated vibrations of love and harmony with divine will to the beavers.

She visited the pond daily, gave True Light, sometimes talking to the beaver and thanking him each time she found no damage. She also checked to see if the note was still visible at the base of the tree. Other Sukyo Mahikari members who spent time at the farm shared in the efforts by offering prayers and radiating True Light around the pond. The beaver remained for about three weeks, but no trees were taken down. Finally, the beaver left.

Years ago, when the first beaver had arrived, the local game warden told Dot and her husband that a beaver never abandons a territory once he finds flowing water and trees for a dam. So Dot was skeptical when she wrote the first note to a beaver asking him to please leave, but she knew that in her Sukyo

Mahikari center they often wrote respectful notes to ants asking them to leave, and they did. Now, years later, the beavers continue to come and go, but Dot's family has not lost another tree and the beavers move on unharmed.

The notes Dot writes to the beavers who come to her pond now are much more respectful and informative than the earlier ones she wrote. This is so important to her effort to grow in humility in her relationship with the beavers, to connect with them more deeply, to communicate with them more clearly and thus grow towards harmony with God. She says, "As with humans, communication with animals should be honest and truthful. When a beaver's perspective is taken into consideration and our need for trees and clean, flowing water for cattle is fully explained, the situation feels in balance. I feel it is this balance that allows for a harmonious solution."

Dot now has a groundhog living under her garden shed, and she's begun writing notes and speaking to him. The animal's tunneling threatens the structural integrity of the building's foundation, revealing to Dot that living in harmony with nature is a constant endeavor requiring respectful awareness on a daily basis. Dot is learning to look at these situations more objectively, with a sincere desire to understand and harmonize with nature when seeking a solution.

Through these experiences, Dot has been able to give True Light, to better explain and demonstrate the teachings to her husband and neighbors, to acknowledge the help of other members who joined her, to maintain the purity of the physical environment, to conduct herself in a calm manner, and to practice humility toward nature. Not only has she been allowed to practice universal principles, but also to see clearly their connectedness. "I am awed by and grateful for this powerful yet humbling awareness," Dot says.

Mirrors of the True Self in Nature

I can relate to Dot's humble awe, as my response to nature has always been to be full of wonder. To suddenly come upon a deer in the forest or a flock of birds in the sky fills me with joy every time. It is one of my innate responses that has endured unchanged from early childhood through adulthood. Connecting with fauna allows me to experience harmony in nature, and to express my soul and spirit's utterly natural sense of renewal and gratitude in response.

Two remarkable encounters occurred long ago before I began giving True Light. One was with a tiger. The other was with two pairs of birds. Since I began giving True Light, I have had many more animal encounters. Over time, integrating spirituality in my daily life has developed my capacity to connect with the deep meaning in such encounters. Grasping meaning in life's experiences, and particularly in profound experiences, increases my joy in living.

I love to tell the story of the tiger I met, face to face, when I was in my early twenties, while studying psychology in graduate school at the University of Delhi in India. During short breaks, I took the opportunity to explore nature preserves near the campus and beyond. One of the places I frequented was the Jim Corbett National Park—a tiger preserve for the Royal Bengal tiger. On one occasion, I managed to persuade two friends to join me. It was a wonderful bus ride to the forest through villages and countryside. In the heart of the park was a simple forest guest house, which we had booked. It was on high ground above a river, so we could observe many animals that came to drink at dawn or dusk.

We saw that the nice forest bungalow beside the guest house had many signs of life. People and cars were coming and going. Upon inquiring what was going on, one of my friends heard that the director of the park was visiting. The director was a close friend of my friend's family, so he invited the three of us up to stop by. The director was very warm and welcoming to all of us. He had another group of young students from other countries with him. Several of the director's staff and a renowned photographer were present too. We learned that the director, his staff, and the photographer were there to work on a tiger conservation initiative called Project Tiger.[13] What could be more exciting?

We were wined and dined and enjoyed a very pleasant evening together. The director invited us to join him and his team at dawn the next morning on their tiger tracking and monitoring expedition. I could think of no better way to explore the bush and learn more about the tiger and its habitat. To my great surprise, my peers were all afraid to go. They chose to sleep in and ride in the director's motorboat the next day instead of joining the tiger expedition.

The next morning at dawn the director and I and a few other people from Project Tiger climbed up on elephants' backs and took off in an elephant convoy. I could view the deep green, lush forest beneath in which the grass itself was much taller than I. After a considerable walk and careful tracking, the director settled on a likely spot. He had a camera and a pair of binoculars. He handed me the binoculars and climbed from the elephant's back to a high branch on a tree. He signaled to me to choose a branch too. I chose a branch closer to the ground where I could still easily make eye contact with the director. The director told me tigers could detect the slightest movement, so I should stay very still. I felt incredibly awed by the opportunity to be there, and I was very excited by the prospect of seeing a tiger face to face.

Meanwhile, our traveling companions moved further into the forest to track and sight a tiger at some other location. The director and I had been sitting there silently for a half an hour or more when the tiger did indeed appear. It was a great and magnificent tiger, and it was carrying a baby buffalo in its jaws. It walked out of the thicket, dropped the limp buffalo carcass on the ground, walked out of the thicket a little further, and sat down in a clearing, relaxed. I was totally amazed and filled with wonder. What a magnificent moment it was! I was sitting on the branch of a tree fifteen feet away from a Royal Bengal tiger, feeling totally present, amazed and filled with joy. I knew this moment was a rare gift, and I savored it completely. At some point I could no longer savor it alone, so I turned my head upwards to catch the director's eye to share the moment and say in silence "How great is this?"

The tiger sensed the slight movement of my head. It became alert and stood up and caught my eye. We looked at each other eye to eye for a few minutes. All I could see was his grandeur. I felt no fear, no panic, no wish to step back. The tiger's eyes were large pools of yellow. I will always remember them. I heard the director click a photograph from his branch above. I knew I had been given much more than I could have ever asked for.

The tiger gave up staring at me and leapt into the tall grass and disappeared. After sitting another half an hour or so, the director decided we should jump off our tree and walk the mile or so back to the guest house. He said the tiger was nearby and would not bother us. When it sensed that we were out of the way, it would return to feast on the buffalo. He said if there was a moment to be afraid of the tiger it was when he noticed us and stood up to face me with his kill nearby. Since he was not going to fight over his kill, we had no reason to fear him, as tigers do not naturally eat humans. Once I was convinced it was safe to do so, I jumped off the tree. The director followed and we walked the half hour or so through the forest with the grass way over our heads to reach the high ground of the guest house.

I recounted the tale to my family. My father said, "You are so lucky!" Years later, I was on the other side of the world in the United States and my parents were in New Delhi at a party where the same wildlife park director was also present. He began telling stories of his experiences with Project Tiger. He told the story of taking a young woman into the forest to see a tiger, saying this was the bravest person he had ever met. My mother realized that he was speaking of me and said, "You must be speaking of our daughter!" Amazed by the symmetry of the connection, the director told my mother he had a gift for her to relay to me. And that is how I received the treasured photograph he had taken of the tiger staring into my eyes.

Engaging with the tiger in the forest that day was unforgettably powerful, and a very great gift. It brought out my true self and helped me to naturally express some of my true attributes, my spiritual presence, love of nature, courage, and joy. It made a memory that will endure through time and serves as a reminder that mirrors of the true self in nature bear witness to our divinity and our true essence. I wasn't at all afraid in the presence of the tiger and my memory of that encounter has stayed with me many years.

I find it most interesting that the month I gave a talk on True Light at the Mindsight Colloquium, the cover of The Economist magazine showed an image of a small domestic cat looking at its reflection the mirror and, instead, seeing a huge tiger. This image goes to the heart of the question. When we see, are we connecting through the true self which is non-material, eternal, wise, deeply connected with all existence, and divine in nature? Or are we seeing through our finite self, connected with some of existence but disconnected from the whole of it? The distance between the two is the journey for most of us: from a life of contribution in material human terms to elevating to fulfill true purpose—thereby living in the flow of continuous joy overflowing to everyone.

Many years after my tiger encounter, I had a most alarming nature experience. I was sitting in the sunroom of our home in Pasadena when I saw something hurtling toward the picture window and then heard a loud thud. I was quite shaken. Fortunately, a workman was working in the backyard. He was startled too and came running. Together we found two dead birds entwined—a red-tailed hawk with a dove in its beak. Both had hit the sunroom picture window at great speed and broken their necks. The workman kindly buried the birds, and I saw the experience as a powerful message to rise to work for peace, to heed heaven's call.

On another day, as I was again alone sitting in the sunroom, two peregrine falcons came. They were huge, powerful birds visiting from the mountains on our horizon. They circled our backyard over and over and over again for about half an hour, then settled on the roof in the back. As before, I experienced the presence of the sacred in a powerful, peaceful form. I felt the visit of a sacred wind in the garden, bringing a great silence and peace. I so wished others could experience this too. My inner sense was utter amazement and joy. Four years later, when I was introduced to Sukyo Mahikari and began giving True Light and learning the universal principles, I had a similar feeling.

Two years or so after I began giving True Light, I was driving home with our two younger children when I received a cell phone call from my older son. His voice was very quiet and full of awe:

"Mom, please come home. There are peacocks in our front yard."

"I am very close," I said, "I will be there momentarily."

When we arrived, all four of us were so gripped by the utter magic of the moment that we silently and quietly came together on the front lawn and sat there. How could there be peacocks in our garden? How did they get here? The peacock family walked about our front yard pecking at seeds in the grass and making themselves at home. We sat for about two hours in complete silence, all of us filled with wonder and joy, feeling no need for words and recognizing beyond all doubt that this was a gift. The peacocks then began exploring our neighbors' gardens. Eventually, they settled in a tree in a neighbor's yard less than a block from our home. Over the past few years, the peacock family has grown. We hear them call in the early mornings and see them as we travel up and down our street. These peacocks, the national bird of India—the land of my birth—now flourish in our California neighborhood.

After I began giving True Light, my father in India began his physical decline. I phoned to check in with him each day. One day, as I was talking with my mother, I looked out the window of the sunroom to see a pure white pigeon sitting on the telephone line. Its rare presence and beautiful unblemished plumage moved me. I remarked to my mother "I see a pure white pigeon on the line at the back. Have you ever seen one?"

"Yes," she said immediately, "I saw one when you were born."

That year, in 2010, the Indian Health Professionals Group of Sukyo Mahikari was established. Sukyo Mahikari staff from the United States and India met with the health professionals. As part of the activities, we visited the Qutb Minar. It is one of the tallest brick minarets in the world, and now a UNESCO World Heritage Site. It was built in 1200 by Qutb-al-Din-Aibak, the founder of the Delhi Sultanate. In the Qutb Complex also stands the non-corroding Iron Pillar, which is thought to have been built by one of the Gupta Emperors in approximately 402 AD. As we were taking in this impressive place, someone mentioned that structures like the towering minaret were constructed by rulers to tune in with God. I noticed once again among a large number of grey and speckled pigeons everywhere, a single pure white pigeon high up on the minaret. I felt joy at the connection and, in a child-like way, pointed the bird out to my friends. They smiled.

I was fifty-one on my first birthday after my father's passing. My mother's gift to me the following year was a book called *Tia*. In my mother tongue, Bengali, tia means parrot. The book tells a spiritual story of a parrot that realizes the truth of self, travels the world, and returns home. Everyone at home is the same, though the parrot is transformed. Soon after I received the book, I was walking on the track at the Caltech gym one evening at sunset when a huge, noisy flock of parrots flew in and filled up a tree by the track. I welcomed the signal of a lively family of parrots returning at sunset to this connected place. It was a wonderful feeling!

Three years later I returned to Honolulu, Hawaii after an absence of twenty-three years, to review the Sukyo Mahikari Intermediate course. One evening as I walked on the beach, I spotted a large flock of pure white pigeons twittering and pecking with joyful energy. Also on this trip, I talked with two colleagues from twenty-three years ago. Four years later they both received the Sukyo Mahikari primary course and began giving True Light at the Honolulu Sukyo Mahikari Center. I see a connection between the sightings of white pigeons I have described and the purpose of True Light in the world. The white pigeons symbolize purity, and True Light is pure as it flows to us from God. Sightings of white pigeons are rare, and True Light provides a rare opportunity to integrate spirituality on the deepest level in daily life.

A couple of years ago I reached out to one of my former graduate students, a dear person and a longtime mental health professional living in Illinois, to tell her about True Light. She immediately visited the Chicago Sukyo Mahikari Center and soon took the primary spiritual development course and, successively, the intermediate and advanced courses. Some time back, she and I were driving to my Pasadena home after giving each other True Light at the Pasadena Sukyo Mahikari Center. As our car passed the peacocks' home on our street, a red-tailed hawk came out of nowhere, swooping down and hovering over our car, traveling with us, until we reached my home. Once again, a bird brought a powerful wind and a peaceful energy with it. We felt awe as we experienced the beauty and marvel of the moment! What a powerfully moving experience and message we received. It felt like coming full circle with birds in this place. Beginning with the experience of a red-tailed hawk and a dove locked in a struggle for survival eighteen years ago, we have ended with the arrival of a wonderful, powerful, peaceful wind trail laid down by a red-tailed hawk bringing a friend of mine and me the message of returning home.

Entering the house after this exhilarating experience, my gaze fell on a little book on the bookshelf—a book I have had since the age of six but had not noticed in a long time. My beloved maternal grandfather gave me this gift. He used to say he had the nonattachment of a bird, and I internalized his message. The title of the book is simply *Birds*, and the cover carries a picture of a red-tailed hawk. How wondrous this experience was, arranged by God and encompassing both my ancestors and nature. I was able to see through my spiritual eye and comprehend more than meets the material eye because of the development of my reflective mind.

Recently, as Mira and David stood beneath the beautiful trees that I described earlier in this chapter, they were discussing how to set up Mira's pottery studio under the trees. Right then a red-tailed hawk flew in and looked at them closely, settling on a branch of the tree as close as ten feet away from them. It kept looking at them and turning its head to look all around. It was not afraid of them at all. David said it was beautiful. Was it saying, "So you are setting up a pottery studio?" I asked Mira. "That is exactly what it was saying!" Mira said. It was Mira's first sighting of a red-tailed hawk up close and at home—such a beautiful, natural continuation of the legacy to resonate with nature. I'm grateful that we have been allowed to see a mirror of the true self in it.

The very next day, Mira and David were in the lumber yard looking for poles to set up a canopy above her pottery wheel. She said there was somehow a feeling of being in India in that lumber yard. Then she noticed a flock of pigeons and among them a few, three or four brown ones among a large flock of grey ones. She saw them flying up and down and noticed their distinctness. "I've been seeing pure white pigeons," I said. "And you now saw some beautiful brown ones." We smiled knowing smiles to each other.

On Mira's birthday this year I gave her a book on the life and work of Salim Ali, who since his birth had a great love of birds. He went on to take a very organic route to becoming India's foremost ornithologist, establishing both the professional and amateur fields of ornithology in India. The cover of the book has a raised image of a large parrot with a bright red head. Lo and behold, soon afterwards, just this species of parrot—and not the smaller ring-necked ones that frequented before—have started flying by our home. They usually come in fours and sometimes in twos. They are very beautiful and periodically chirpy birds. And lately monarch butterflies have begun fluttering around me almost every time I step outdoors!

Seeing Through Our Spiritual Eyes

When I was allowed to see my true self and experience its divine energy (as I related in chapter one), I saw that it is distinct from my mind, which is distinct from my body, though they all interconnect. This was an early moment of seeing through my spiritual eyes when I was still new in my daily spiritual practice and in my effort to harmonize myself and my family with God. I realize that true commitment is itself elevating, however new it is. As the mind is purified by divine Light and consistent, sincere efforts are made to elevate daily life to harmonize with divine principles, the mind is gradually illuminated by the torchlight of the soul. In my experience, every effort to harmonize oneself with God and elevate spiritually through actions like reviewing spiritual development courses, primary, intermediate or advanced, attending study classes, offering overnight center security service or, as in this time of COVID-19 pandemic, offering security service during the day and night at closed centers, goes toward shining the torchlight of the soul through the mind. Feelings of warmth toward others and within the body, sense of well-being, happiness and elevation fill experience. Seeing through our spiritual eyes is cultivated. The vibration of this seeing is always serene and has a vastness and selfless quality to it that fills the heart with a pure form of happiness. We can develop as human beings to see the world through the window of the soul slowly and step by step. We can begin to grasp divine truths for ourselves and progressively elevate our innermost attitude to immovable alignment with God, progressing in purity and righteousness toward wholeness and holiness.

Another powerful early experience of seeing through my spiritual eyes took place in India. I was traveling with my family in the Himalaya along the river Ganges to two holy sites, Hardwar and Rishikesh. With gratitude, we settled into a beautiful place for the night by the flowing river Ganges with the Shivalik ranges of the lower Himalaya on the horizon. Our rooms had ceiling to floor glass on a whole wall, allowing us a magnificent view of the river and mountains. In the early dawn, I felt a gentle wind nudge me on my left shoulder. I awakened to see a most beautiful vision of a crescent moon glistening above the peaks of the Shivalik mountains. In Hinduism the crescent moon is associated with the deity Shiva, who is depicted wearing the crescent on his forehead. And so, I was awoken to witness in silence a great, ineffable presence of Shiva in the Shivalik ranges as my family lay fast asleep all around me. "Ah, so this is why these mountains are called the Shivaliks, because Shiva resides in them," I whispered. In the crisp, clear, still air of dawn I sat up to savor this magnificent experience. Refreshed by grasping this deep meaning, I went back to sleep.

Like so many others, prior to a committed daily practice of Light giving and divine principles, I developed my mind's socio-emotional abilities and neural circuitry through life experiences, education, and work. This helped me interiorize learning to build and use capacities for self-awareness, empathy, compassion, and kindness. Along with this, I also developed my mind's cognitive abilities and neural circuitry that helped me externalize learning using logical, technical, critical thinking, and organizational/executive functioning abilities. Integrating these capacities through reflection and relationships has contributed to my well-being, as Dan Siegel's work in IPNB has taught me.

Now elevating my mind through daily efforts in divine service and developing my mind's reflective capacity in my Circles group helps me penetrate deeper spiritual and sometimes divine meaning in relationships and events that occur in everyday life. My felt experience of the vibration of my innermost attitude and those of others with whom I communicate has become available and accessible to me. Through this felt connection with my innermost attitude and true self, I have the opportunity to reflect and perceive progressive depths of spiritual and divine meaning in everyday life experiences and interactions. I experience my mind growing towards true harmony in my inner depths. The serenity and purity that emanates continues to allow access to deeper meaning. This fruit of spiritual practice is what my Circles team members and I hope to give to leaders and all people in small, warm organic groups of teams and families. In the process of self-training, now we hope to bring people the experience of Light and reflection to glimpse felt connection with God, with innermost attitude and true self and with the torchlight of the soul illuminating the mind, the whole world and all relationships with it. This inner road to reclaim our true destiny, our divinity, and our harmony with nature for posterity is our big dream.

If I'm paying attention, little messages from the divine arrive every day. For example, about a month ago a neighbor stopped by to say that a bobcat was sitting in their backyard, to watch out for it as it may decide to visit ours. My friend who lives close by also mentioned the bobcat walking around on her street earlier in the day. Sure enough, a little later we saw a beautiful ochre brown, lean, and muscular bobcat in our backyard showing us its back only. I felt its strong, pure energy though, and was quite elated. It settled down and spent some time in our backyard before slipping away, but only after leaving its calling card in the place the new building to welcome holy Goshintai is to come.

Fast forward a month to the present time. Great fires are raging not far away and the one near us has been named "the bobcat fire." In the depths of my heart I felt the vibration of deep gratitude for God's great love in purifying the environment, awakening us spiritually to live in deeper harmony with nature and preparing our family and area to welcome holy Goshintai in the near future. I also felt apology for having to awaken through so much purification and make extra daily efforts in prayer and radiating Light to the environment with my family to the spirit realm of the fires.

As I reflected on our effort at the Pasadena Center to step up members' commitment to purifying the air as the air quality is so low with the fires, a staff member called me at the center to ask for updates on guidance in response to the fires. I relayed that we were guided to offer prayers and give Light to the environment morning and night. I also shared my deep personal gratitude for the purification which I see as a means to awaken as many of us as possible to living daily life in deeper harmony with nature. She shared her prayer of apology for the contamination of our souls to have to come to awakening through such purification.

I remember eleven years ago there were fires on the San Gabriel Mountains that face the Pasadena Center. There was a youth member taking care of the center alone, as most members (including me) were at the Los Angeles Center for the intermediate spiritual development course. The young man saw great flames on the mountain coming dangerously close to the center. He prayed deeply and stood resolutely at the entrance of the center, radiating Light and chanting the prayer of purification. Within moments, the direction of the winds changed and the flames facing the center tempered. He witnessed the divine truth that the spiritual realm and physical realms can be purified by divine Light in place of physical purification. I think being motivated by deep care reclaims our humanity allowing us to walk together towards reclaiming our divinity, the Light within. In Bengali (my mother tongue) there is a word for precious care. It is called jotno. I love the word, its vibration, the attitude it engenders, and its meaning.

Just recently a bobcat appeared in our backyard! It looked like a young one. It was moving through the grass quickly when I called out "Welcome" and began radiating Light. It turned around, went back into our yard and then left. I mentioned the bobcat visits and the name of the fire that is raging in the mountains to an old college friend in India who is also a Light giver. He interprets it as a divine message. I also mentioned the same to a staff member at the Pasadena Center and she said this place where we are living closer to the mountains may have been the bobcats' habitat and home at one time. She said though they have to experience the bad air during this purification while we can shelter indoors, they will be happy when the Light increases with the arrival of holy Goshintai. It is this happiness and flourishment of nature and ourselves together that we must seek and we will naturally embody as true stewards of earth as we grow spiritually. It is imperative for us as a human family at the threshold of irreversible climate change to harmonize with God through spiritual practice, elevation of mind and innermost attitude to accomplish true harmony in spirit, mind, and body in our daily lives. I thus felt honored and moved to find a sole dove hovering at my kitchen window a few days ago as the morning sunlight streamed in. What a wonderful visit, filling my heart with warmth and hope.

Chapter 4

Spotlights

Girish Chandorkar

These are words of profound wisdom with an underlying message of altruistic love for humanity and the environment in its myriad forms. If this attitude permeates our lives, we will elevate our spiritual selves and live in harmony with the divine plan. The message is truly inspiring as we see how normal human beings can attain spiritual upliftment without resorting to esoteric practices. Faith, humility, and gratitude—while forsaking greed and a self-centered attitude, is the way to achieve spiritual peace.

Dekila Chungyalpa

This chapter is an important reminder that we acknowledge that the earth is a closed system and whatever we do to the earth comes back upon ourselves. We teeter at the edge of several kinds of ecological destruction and are close to crossing earth system thresholds such as climate change and biodiversity loss. Once we cross over, many of the physical feedback mechanisms will no longer be reversible or stable and we will doom ourselves along with so many other living parts of this marvelous planet. And yet, as Leena Banerjee Brown demonstrates, the earth is fundamentally compassionate – each of her creations are functionally and aesthetically integral and all that is needed for us humans to reverse the enormous environmental damage and self-harm we have indulged in is to open up to that connection and root ourselves spiritually, mindfully, and physically to the land we live upon. She offers her life evidence that this can be done, as we read her story and write our own.

Deepa Bhushan

It has been an enlightening experience to read this spiritual journey with Sukyo Mahikari, and eye opening to see the depth in Leena's relationship with her near and dear ones and her surroundings. The way she grew vegetables and cooked with total mindfulness brought out the qualities of the food to be eaten. The experiences of Roger Beck and yoko farming show how important this harmony between humans and nature is. People who live in cities and highrise buildings don't realize how much harm the disconnect from earth is doing to them. The way our spirit wakes up and soothes the mind and the body when we live next to the earth is beautifully shown through the stories Leena has shared. Nature teaches us to be grateful for every beautiful day and the harmony in nature creates humility in us. The spirit of cooperation we witness in nature, in the gardens, jungles, and natural farms is the way forward for humanity. It is the only way we will be able to survive without hatred and competition. To live with gratefulness, humility, and acceptance of one's circumstances we have to tap into our inner selves, and this is much easier if we are able to live in nature and learn from our surroundings.

Sara Edrington, PsyD and Sean Edrington

We enter mega supermarkets and leave unsatiated as nourishment manifests from harmony, where food sources, flora, and one's spirit are honored. Leena's words inspire us to meet our responsibility to life, to God. When motivated by deep care, embracing gratitude, our joyous vibrations reach others in a way our frantic efforts cannot. Her message is reassuring—a symbiotic relationship with nature will be met with spiritual growth. This chapter initiated our own recounting and relishing the interconnection between our child selves and nature. Like her father, Leena "offers splashes of color" through her anecdotes and wisdom that nourish hope and guide humanity.

Chapter 5

Growing Together in Wisdom

s we develop together in the flow of Light, illumining our minds, we are allowed to live harmoniously with nature and among our fellow humans. As we commit to daily practice, we become spiritually mature and naturally begin to live in tune with God and universal principles such as altruistic love, gratitude, humility, and acceptance of divine will. Our seeking grows in selflessness and true self-awareness, turning away from the self-centeredness of messages, habits, and practices rampant in the world today. We absorb the high vibrations of Light into our souls with great gratitude and joy. We uplift our innermost attitudes and motives that lead us to make others' burdens lighter, others' happiness our own. Our souls naturally shine Light into the circles of our lives, making each more beautiful and complete—gradually peerless, gradually immeasurable, gradually endless. We grow together in wisdom towards a peaceful world in which we are in tune with God and in harmony with nature, each other, and the technologies that help us navigate life.

In this fifth and final chapter, I'd like to fine-tune the aperture of the lens through which we observe the ups and downs prevalent in every person's life by zeroing in on several specific personal accounts of how individual lives have been transformed by the spiritual practices associated with Sukyo Mahikari. And then I'd like to open that aperture to a wide-angle view of the global invitation to seek spiritual development. The ability to see both the micro and the macro as we observe life and collect the data and inner wisdom upon which we choose our life's priorities is an important development of the spirit-mind-body approach to life.

I hope the following accounts resonate with your own stories of things you may have experienced. Material-first culture often censors the empirically inexplicable elements of life, from the tiny miracles we glimpse as we witness a simple sunrise, to profound reversals of medical conditions that even the most skeptical hospital cultures cannot deny or explain. When we start to share the stories from our own families and friends, others who have been silenced or shamed by material-first culture begin to speak their truths. Perhaps you will be emboldened to think of your own life's unexpected, unexplainable moments of grace as you read these accounts.

As a Sukyo Mahikari practitioner who is committed to universal principles, my spiritual practices are framed by giving and receiving True Light. And so, the stories in this chapter are similarly framed. But they are also part of a larger dynamic of spirit-first communities that share a commitment to following God's will, whatever name a given community may ascribe to the divine. Various spiritual traditions and movements hold equally miraculous accounts of spiritual transformation and upliftment, with similar accounts of physical manifestations thereof. I hope you will draw upon your own tradition as you experience these miraculous stories from Sukyo Mahikari, and then join with me in exploring the larger context from which this era of spiritual awakening flows.

True Light and the Miracle of Life

As we focus our attention on improvements in well-being, including both physical and mental health, we will explore how spiritual practice can change and brighten lives, awakening and inspiring us to grow together in wisdom. Many of the people involved in these case studies are True Light practitioners I have come to know on my journey with Sukyo Mahikari, some of whom have been given different names to preserve their anonymity.

Life itself is miraculous. The more we recognize this, the more we see that life is imbued with purpose and filled with opportunities to contribute to the collective development and well-being of all, as well as fulfillment of individual destiny. The following case studies, made available to me by physicians who are also Sukyo Mahikari practitioners, bring home the preciousness of life as they document the harmonious balance between the medical and the miraculous. I will leave it to you, dear reader, to discern the greater meaning of these stories as they speak to your heart. I share these specific stories because they reveal the importance of incorporating spiritual practice in the medical professions, reinforcing the reality that medical treatment and spiritual practice are complementary.

I'd like to begin with some stories shared by my friend Dr. Jaya Lalmohan, who along with her husband Balamurali Lalmohan, runs Shantigram Wellness Centre in the Idukki district of Kerala, India. Their mission is to impart holistic medical service and training to their community and nurture spirit-centered youth. They offer the use of their home as a Sukyo Mahikari center and also offer service together at the close-by Kochi Sukyo Mahikari Center. Prior to Shantigram, Jaya served the state of Kerala's health services for several decades and later the Government of India's Ministry of Health. She trained physicians in maternal and child health, collaborating in international projects as well. Devoted Sukyo Mahikari practitioners, Jaya and her husband have helped many family members and friends practice True Light giving and the universal principles. Jaya shared two beautiful experiences with me, changing her patients' names to preserve their anonymity.

A woman we will call Uma began bleeding profusely immediately after giving birth in the hospital where Jaya headed the maternity department. As her body went into shock, Uma had no pulse and no blood pressure and froth was coming out of her mouth. She did not respond to physical stimuli as the medical staff tried to revive her, and large doses of intravenous drugs did not stop the bleeding. Bewildered at the impending death of a woman who had just given birth normally to a healthy baby, the attending physicians called Jaya (their supervisor) to the maternity ward STAT. As soon as she reached the patient's room, Jaya began radiating True Light continuously to Uma's head, abdomen, and chest. After receiving True Light for ten or fifteen minutes, Uma's breathing became regular, her bleeding stopped, she responded to stimuli, her blood pressure became steady, she opened her eyes and looked around, and her face was bright. The next morning, Jaya was surprised to hear Uma say that when she was receiving True Light and regaining consciousness, she saw angels descend on her body. Uma showed no apparent effects from the previous day's heavy bleeding, and she was able to feed and care for her newborn baby. Jaya's response: "Anything is possible if one surrenders and tunes in to the profound depths of truth accessible through True Light."

In another maternity case, Jaya shared with me the miracle of life and True Light—this time through a newborn baby. A pregnant woman experiencing hypertension and premature onset of labor was attended by a gynecologist at the hospital where Jaya had previously worked. An emergency caesarean section was performed. Sadly, the baby, a boy, was underweight, bluish, and had no heartbeat. Standard measures of resuscitation such as suction of the air passages, administering oxygen, respiratory stimulant injection, and other medical measures did not initiate respiration in the baby. He was declared dead before Jaya, who had been called to assist the gynecologist, could get to him. But knowing the influence of True Light on the interrelated spirit, mind, and body of a person, Jaya ignored the death pronouncement and immediately began radiating True Light to the lifeless baby. After five to seven minutes, the bluish color disappeared from his skin and the baby began crying feebly. All present were astonished and deeply moved to see the baby begin to breathe on his own after being declared deceased! Medicines were administered to prevent infection, and the little boy—named Kartik—was wrapped in warm blankets and taken to the intensive care unit. The next day when Jaya checked on him in the ICU, Kartik appeared quite normal as his smiling mother nursed him. The mother had seen Jaya give True Light to her baby and thanked her profusely for saving her baby's life. This unexpected return to life also awakened the doctors and staff in the ICU and operating theatre units to the importance of the realm of spirit to their work.

Kartik was discharged from the hospital after five days. Two years later, his mother entered Jaya's office and introduced herself and the bright-eyed boy she held in her arms saying, "Do you remember this child? He is the child you saved with prayers!" Kartik was perfectly healthy and bubbling with energy. There was no evidence of birth asphyxia (damage caused by oxygen deprivation before, during, and immediately after birth). For Jaya, Kartik's miraculous resuscitation is living proof that spirit is primary. Purification of the spirit in this case changed the arrangement from the spirit leaving to remaining in the body. The rejuvenation of spirit reflected rejuvenation of the mind and body at birth and thereafter. Jaya felt awe, surprise, and gratitude for the love and power in True Light, as she deepened her commitment to apply this principle in the practice of medicine.

While still serving the government of India in New Delhi, Jaya had the opportunity to help her immediate superior, a pediatrician named Dr. M.S. Jayalakshmi, receive Light. Jayalakshmi now practices True Light at the

New Delhi Sukyo Mahikari Center. Here's the background story behind how Jayalakshmi became attuned to the spiritual dimension of her work in pediatrics.

As Jayalakshmi's daughter was preparing to give birth, the fetal heart rate monitor signaled fetal distress, so a caesarean section was performed. The baby, Jayalakshmi's granddaughter, was admitted to the neonatal ICU of a teaching hospital in New Delhi due to low birth weight and moderate asphyxia. The baby's respiratory distress continued during the week following birth, at which point her condition rapidly deteriorated and became critical. At this time a congenital cystic lung condition was detected by a medical team including a pediatric physician, pediatric surgeon, and radiologist. This resulted in the seven-day-old infant undergoing lung surgery to locate the cysts with follow up plans to remove any affected lobes. However, the surgery revealed no cysts— only secretions and air pockets caused by vigorous resuscitation in the days preceding surgery, but the baby remained in the neonatal intensive care unit (NICU) for twenty-eight days.

Jaya gave the infant True Light every day she was in the NICU, during which time her condition gradually improved. For the next two months the newborn baby continued to receive True Light daily. At that point, Jayalakshmi—moved by the positive effects of True Light on her baby granddaughter's life—received the Sukyo Mahikari primary spiritual development course and became a True Light practitioner herself. She then took responsibility for giving her granddaughter True Light each day and began offering service at the Sukyo Mahikari New Delhi Center.

At nine months of age, Jayalakshmi's granddaughter began to show symptoms of mild cerebral impairment, so a brain scan and a kidney scan were recommended. Jayalakshmi's family stayed focused on giving True Light, holding off on further diagnostics for a short period of time. Accepting medical diagnosis and treatment as part of God's arrangements, they decided to combine the practice of True Light with medical recommendations, as is encouraged in Sukyo Mahikari practice. And so, they were overwhelmed with gratitude when any sign of cerebral impairment disappeared one month after it was first noticed. At age two, a urinary problem Jayalakshmi's granddaughter had experienced since birth also disappeared. At two years and five months, Jayalakshmi's granddaughter was a bundle of joy, bubbling with life and affection for all, a beautiful child who loves to pray to God with her ninety-seven-year-old great grandfather. Although she is now of slight build and below normal weight, Jayalakshmi's granddaughter is achieving her developmental milestones normally.

While it's difficult to imagine what Jayalakshmi went through as a pediatrician with a pediatric emergency like her granddaughter's so close to home, I am deeply grateful she has become one of the many physicians I know who are combining their medical training with studying the principles of Sukyo Mahikari, devoting significant time and energy to service at a Sukyo Mahikari Center and giving people True Light.

When members of my own family have been injured or ill, I've been deeply grateful to give them True Light, for their giving each other True Light, and for other Light Givers who have helped them. I have also incorporated my spiritual practice in my professional life. As a psychologist with significant experience in treating infants, young children, and families who have experienced trauma, you might imagine I have seen some rather tragic cases over the course of my career. This is true. I rarely speak about the details of my work unless I'm guiding students or supervising other psychologists. But for the purposes of showing how True Light can penetrate the depths of such work, I will break my silence with the following real-life examples, once again, changing names to preserve anonymity.

Bringing Mental Health into the Light

Alejandra was eight years old when she began seeing a therapist who was under my supervision. She experienced intense anxiety, constant inner terror, and emotional isolation each day. As you might imagine, her school performance was significantly affected. After several years of chronic and traumatic exposure to domestic violence, including personal physical, emotional, and sexual abuse by a male perpetrator, she had intense anxiety, inner terror, and emotional isolation resulting from reliving her emotional traumas and abusive events. She had nightmares several times per week and frequent flashbacks while awake. She even feared that her perpetrator would find her at school and hurt her, sometimes mistaking her male teacher's voice and face to be that of her perpetrator.

Thankfully, Alejandra was eager to participate in therapy. She established a working relationship with her therapist in the first session and began art therapy to access her traumas. Her drawings vividly expressed her internal world and emotional struggles. This helped her to regulate her emotions and process her traumatic experiences, allowing her to touch the feelings and step back from them when she felt overwhelmed. Alejandra's therapist followed her lead—seeing, normalizing, and validating Alejandra's emotional experiences. She helped Alejandra open up and express her emotional pain. This led to joint reflections and the discovery of new and positive meaning. Art became the avenue for Alejandra to delve into her spirit and subconscious mind. The therapeutic relationship made the pain bearable and available for exploration of meaning. Through these reflections and the sharing of underlying meaning in her traumatic experiences, Alejandra released her bodily symptoms and feelings of terror.

The spiritual core of Alejandra's treatment came through her psychotherapist, who had asked me, as her clinical supervisor, to give her True Light before each weekly supervision meeting. Alejandra's psychotherapist found that receiving True Light gave her profound experiences of connection with her own spirit, mind, and body. True Light energized her, elevated her innermost attitude and vibration, and made her more emotionally available to her patients. Her humanity and compassion came to the fore. As a result, she could connect very deeply with Alejandra during their therapy sessions. She could quickly tune in and grasp Alejandra's emotional process to help her deeply explore and express it in her drawings and in processing her feelings. Alejandra frequently became stuck, expressing feelings of helplessness and powerlessness. Because receiving True Light attuned the psychotherapist to the positive vibrations in her soul, she felt she had access to more mental and emotional resources, and more attuned responses to help Alejandra break free of trauma's grasp. In this way, together they were able to move smoothly through inner turmoil to resolution.

By giving True Light to the psychotherapist, I also became present to a deeper sense of warmth, connection, and harmony with my supervisee, which enhanced an already empathic, productive relationship. The quality of insights that arose in our clinical supervision dialogue became more deeply positive and very moving. This quality of understanding also helped the psychotherapist help Alejandra move ahead when she became stuck. The psychotherapist told me that receiving True Light helped her to be a clear mirror for Alejandra. She felt awakened to her soul, her true self. "I am not my experiences; I am not my fear, I am Light, I am whole, I am safe," she said. Each time she received True Light, she connected with the positive vibrations in the depths of her true self and felt a great sense of connectedness to everyone—to what Dan Siegel calls the "we-self." She could mirror and transmit this presence to Alejandra with truth and power. As a result, Alejandra moved from foster care to successful reunification with her mother. Alejandra's inner terror and anxiety are now alleviated, allowing her to lead a well-adjusted life.

In another case in which I was invited to consult I met Akio, an adult male who suffers from paranoid schizophrenia. Akio's parents—who are Sukyo Mahikari practitioners—requested, in accordance with the guidance of the director of their Sukyo Mahikari center, that a psychologist on the treatment team receive True Light. So, prior to his weekly meeting with the family, the psychologist treating Akio began receiving True Light at the Sukyo Mahikari center for fifty minutes.

The psychologist described himself as a skeptic who receives True Light in order to be sensitive to the culture of Akio and his family. He has shared his approach with his colleagues on the treatment team but feels silenced and unable to have substantive discussion with these peers, who show no interest in spirituality or the art of True Light. Without better understanding of this spiritual practice among peers, he fears he might be removed from the treatment team. That would leave Akio and his family without culturally sensitive help.

Akio's medication and behavioral treatment are monitored through regularly scheduled meetings by the treatment team, with the goal of gradually lowering the level of care Akio needs. The psychologist feels that western medicine offers little hope in cases such as Akio's. By joining the family in their practice of Sukyo Mahikari and combining this with conventional psychiatric-psychological medicine, he feels he is offering them the best available treatment, which gives them real hope for long-term success.

Over the past six years, Akio's situation has stabilized and the family is hopeful. This has been achieved through the efforts of Akio and his family, assisted by staff of the Sukyo Mahikari Center and the treatment team, giving and receiving True Light, applying universal principles in daily life, and following medical treatment protocols. The spiritual dimension of Akio's treatment was enhanced by attending and re-attending the Sukyo Mahikari primary and intermediate spiritual development courses. Guidance given by Sukyo Mahikari staff members was another important spur to progress, facilitating spiritual realizations and elevation of consciousness.

The psychologist has encouraged Akio's family to become active in the National Alliance on Mental Illness, including its Care and Share groups. Akio's family recently invited two other families from Care and Share to a Sukyo Mahikari center open house, where they heard about the art of True Light and universal principles. They received True Light and talked with Akio's psychologist. They understood that progress by Akio and his family has been accelerated through combining Sukyo Mahikari with the efforts of a team of medical professionals.

Sukyo Mahikari practitioners often notice that when they shift their focus away from their personal problems toward helping others, their personal circumstances spontaneously and mysteriously improve. Making other families from Care and Share aware of Sukyo Mahikari reflects this shift toward helping others. Akio's family has expressed that by taking these steps together, they have elevated from living with constant fear and anxiety to experiencing an inner sense of true calm and hope for the future. They said this is why they are enthusiastic about encouraging families facing chronic mental health problems to experience, know, and practice Sukyo Mahikari—and to combine it with treatment by their mental health practitioners.

Not every case is as extreme as Alejandra's and Akio's. As a Sukyo Mahikari practitioner and professional psychologist on a visit to India, I was asked to consult with Tia, a young professional Indian woman who was experiencing anxiety and mild depression after the untimely death of her mother and a failed romantic relationship. She felt tense, was easily irritated, made impulsive decisions, was judgmental toward others, and had withdrawn into a shell. I grasped Tia's condition, psychologically and spiritually, and communicated this psychological assessment and understanding in the form of a prayer offered to God jointly with her. Because Tia also is a Sukyo Mahikari practitioner, I recommended that she be active and thorough in her practice of giving True Light. I also suggested short-term psychotherapy with local practitioners, but she chose to rely instead on the psychological assessment and guidance she received from me.

At the end of one discussion I had with Tia, I stood with her for a few moments in silence. I then expressed out loud my deep, empathic understanding of her condition and feelings, gratitude for the way this cleansing gave her an opportunity to elevate her soul and spirit, and apology for the spiritual causes of her emotional suffering. I expressed the hope that her challenges would open the way for deeper understanding of their meaning and bring her freedom and fulfillment in life.

Tia experienced connection through the prayer. To her, the vibrations in these reflections were deep, positive, and powerfully supportive. She took to heart the realization that all the emotional pain she had undergone was an opportunity for her to elevate in spirit. With this deep realization and sense of inner responsibility, she felt moved and grateful. She committed herself more deeply to the practice of giving True Light and increased her volunteer hours at the New Delhi Sukyo Mahikari Center, as well as her participation in center activities. Her spiritual practice and interaction with fellow practitioners led her to greater awareness of her true self, deepening her feelings of gratitude and humility. She experienced what a difference a smile could make in her life.

A friend who had come into her life at her workplace helped her emerge from her shell. She also helped her lose extra pounds, improving both her health and her confidence. Tia's face began to glow! Her friend helped her realize the need to change the negative aspects of her innermost consciousness, as reflected in her quick temper and criticism of others. With these changes, Tia's humility and consideration for others grew. She then understood that patience and love are needed for relationships to grow and improve. Giving and receiving True

Light helped her gain inner perspective, elevate her vibration, and grow in her sincere desire to help others. A True Light practitioner from another city visited Tia and helped her understand how to think beyond her own convenience and become more selfless in offering divine service. Consequently, Tia began to visit the New Delhi Sukyo Mahikari Center even more frequently, whenever her work schedule allowed.

A year and a half later, Tia felt peaceful, calm, and stable in her frame of mind. She felt gratitude for all she has, as well as for the circumstances she encounters as she moves through her day. The vibration of her soul thus elevated, she could enjoy the small things in life. She is grateful for many blessings—having a car, reaching the office on time, returning home safely every day, and having a good night's sleep. She has abandoned her feelings of grudge and resentment toward the person with whom she had a failed romantic relationship. She is grateful for his constant support during her mother's illness, but now realizes it was an expression of his love for her as a friend, rather than a soul mate. She saw the manifestation of God's great love in leading her to work in the important field of conservation, in acquainting her with her workplace friend, and in arranging her work hours so she could comfortably balance work with household responsibilities in support of her father.

No longer impulsive or judgmental, Tia humbly and openly tries to understand others' points of view. She is better able to deal with her anxiety, and recently Tia has found her true soul mate. Her fiancé's family is very loving toward her such that she feels loved as a daughter by both her future mother-in-law and future father-in-law. This love is more than she ever expected. Tia is happy that her soul mate shares her profession, something else she had not expected. He is a caring person like herself, has accepted her devotion to the practice of True Light, visits the Center with her in New Delhi and Singapore, and has begun receiving True Light. Tia is very grateful and very happy.

True Light and Enhanced Well-being

There are numerous examples of Sukyo Mahikari practitioners in many parts of the world who combine Light giving with medical or psychological interventions to help people increase their well-being. One such effort moved me very much when I learned of it. It is the example of a small, systematic study by Dr. Takahiro Ochi of the University of Osaka Medical School where he serves as physician and professor. He initially treated his arthritis patients with only allopathic medicine. However, because of the considerable side effects experienced by his patients, he arranged for some of them to be treated with herbal medicine, which causes fewer side effects. The herbal treatments were more effective for patients with mild forms of arthritis, but neither allopathic nor herbal medical treatments stopped the progression of joint destruction.

As he continued searching for better ways to help his patients, Takahiro encountered a rheumatoid arthritis patient in an advanced condition who was unusually bright and cheerful. The patient was not taking any kind of medication but had a daily practice of giving and receiving True Light. This was Takahiro's introduction to Sukyo Mahikari.

At the Sukyo Mahikari Center, Takahiro met more rheumatoid arthritis patients who were active practitioners of True Light. Their conditions ranged from mild to severe rheumatoid arthritis, and none of them was being prescribed any type of medication by their doctor. Each was bright and cheerful, and their innermost attitude was deeply positive and grateful. Their well-being was reflected in an especially good face scale index—the method by which many of you may have rated the intensity of your pain by selecting the appropriate facial expression on a series of emoji drawings—in sharp contrast to Takahiro's more typical arthritis patients.[14]

Takahiro tracked sixteen True-Light-practicing rheumatoid arthritis patients over a five-year period, asking Sukyo Mahikari staff members about the details of each patient's spiritual practice. Based on his interpretation of these details, he rated each person's quality of practice in four categories—level of spiritual impurity, innermost attitude, True Light practice, and other forms of service to God at the Sukyo Mahikari center. Takahiro relied upon his own observation to classify each patient as free walking, supported walking, or unable to walk. The data showed that higher quality-of-practice ratings were correlated with higher quality of life, including greater mobility.

Takahiro found that enthusiastic True Light practitioners experienced intense pain in the first three months after committing themselves to divine service, followed by marked pain reduction as they were allowed to overcome the deep negative karma associated with their pain. Reduction in pain may have caused them to become brighter in their attitudes and outlook, but Takahiro speculated that the improvement in the disease itself was also due to the more positive innermost attitude and outlook. Further, those patients with mild arthritis had fewer difficulties in daily life when compared with patients who were not Sukyo Mahikari practitioners. Those with severe arthritis were still able to function with the support of family and members of their Sukyo Mahikari community. All the True-Light-practicing patients maintained bright, cheerful attitudes and vibrations. They did not require medication for pain or inflammation. The existence of this observational connection between spirit, mind, and body, together with the empirical evidence documenting it, astonished Takahiro. He realized that the spiritual dimension, which often lies beyond modern medicine, "is of deep significance to humanity."

Roger Beck personally relates to Dr. Takahiro Ochi's study in relation to his own experience. When Roger was first diagnosed with rheumatoid arthritis, his doctor's recommended treatment was ineffective. For several years, Roger sought many alternative arthritis remedies, all of which were also ineffective. But things began to change when he first received True Light and became a Sukyo Mahikari spiritual practitioner about three months later.

Physical symptoms did not change immediately, but Roger began, step by step, to increase his spiritual practice and his spirits began to lift in spite of his rheumatoid arthritis. Once, when attending a Sukyo Mahikari training seminar in Los Angeles, Roger's smile was chosen by the participants as the most radiant among those attending—perhaps similar to Dr. Ochi's findings with the face scale index of his rheumatoid arthritis patients who were Sukyo Mahikari practitioners. Over time, as his forms of service to God and others broadened and their frequency increased, Roger's symptoms—as previously recounted—completed disappeared.

So, as you can see, Sukyo Mahikari is not primarily intended to be a method by which people receive cures to illness or disease. Giving and receiving True Light helps elevate the mind of the practitioner, reorienting them to a spirit-first way of life as they offer sincere gratitude for the ups and downs, the cleansings and the blessings, and refocus their attention on service to God and others. It is through this reorientation of life and deep connection with God in the realm of spirit by each person taking responsibility to actively purify the spirit through divine service and gratitude for cleansings and blessings alike that the physical realm is influenced and transformed. The divine service of a person and their spiritual elevation thus helps them and also brings many divine blessings and arrangements to related and connected souls. Such is the expansive nature of God's love and arrangement of three-dimensional or spirit-mind-body medicine.

Intuitive Spirit-Mind-Body Health

My daughter Mira has an interesting story involving her health and well-being. As a Sukyo Mahikari practitioner from the very young age of eleven, Mira had an inexplicable awareness about a dental situation that provides an excellent illustration of the insight that often accompanies practicing True Light. I'd like to share it here in her own words, as she retells it in this autobiographical account:

"I knew my teeth were distinctly mine from a very young age—each one was deeply rooted, and fervently eager to stay with me long past when my peers lost their baby teeth. My dentists took note of my developmental delay and insisted on close monitoring. I understood their vigilance, yet I also sensed their anxiety. I experienced their fear instead of their support and trust in my body's process. Instead of seeing a healthy but unique patient, the assumption was there was something wrong that needed to be fixed. Even at a young age, I knew better than to react to something natural with fear.

But years passed and only a few of my teeth had fallen out naturally. Since my remaining baby teeth appeared unwilling to leave on their own, when I was about eleven I underwent a series of surgeries to remove some of them. But even then, my permanent teeth did not move into position promptly, and some were not located where they could do so easily. Both my pediatric dentist and my orthodontist viewed my situation as severe. They wanted to use braces to correct my idiosyncratic mouth. I discussed braces with both of them several times. From their perspective, failing to follow their advice would compromise both my overall dental health and future happiness.

When I left my pediatric dentist's office the last time, I found myself able to say in words what I had felt all along. For the blessing of this insight and the ability to voice it I am deeply grateful. I told my mother I didn't feel the recommended procedures were necessary, and that, one way or another, my teeth would be alright. To my amazement, my mother connected with what I said and accepted it completely. We shared a moment of deep clarity between us. My father accepted the position my mother and I had come to. So, my parents and I decided to wait, calmly and with confidence.

Although the doctors' well-meaning recommendations were in line with standard practice, they didn't really know us or connect with us personally. So, they couldn't possibly understand our hesitation to follow their recommendation. As givers of True Light, my parents and I were allowed to experience and see beyond the physical to the deeper interconnected dimensions of spirit, mind, and body. We understood the deep cleansing of my spiritual aspect I was going through was manifesting in the condition of my mouth, which we recognized as a natural step toward a better overall outcome. I continued to give and receive True Light, do my best to practice the universal principles, and grow spiritually.

Looking back, I can't explain logically why I was so confident as an eleven-year-old in rejecting recommendations from my pediatric dentist and my orthodontist. Similarly, I can't explain why my mother readily accepted my conclusion the instant I verbalized it. However, both of us were awake spiritually and attuned to deeper truth that allowed us to be confident, calm and sure as we relied on our connection with divine wisdom to make an important choice.

Slowly, my teeth straightened out, though a slight overcrowding remained. Until recently, I thought that would be the end of my story. But, as is often the case, a combination of attunement to God and wise medical counsel is the answer. More recently I learned that the slight crowding of my teeth was a symptom of an underlying cause. It was resolved by conducting a frenulectomy to unhitch a constraint in my tongue so it can exert more outward force in my mouth, plus the use of a simple, gentle, and non-invasive osteopathic device to stimulate bone growth in my jaw. As my jawbone begins to grow, my teeth will naturally find the room needed to overcome the crowding. No braces or retainers of any form are needed.

I see even more clearly now that at the age of eleven I was being guided with love, helping me to learn the importance of placing my faith in God. Faith and my active spiritual practice of giving True Light and applying universal principles were quite likely the pre-condition for the initial straightening of my teeth, followed by *the recent arrangement of a gentle, natural, long-term solution for correcting my slight overcrowding. I am profoundly grateful for the blessing I received, as well as the chance to more deeply understand the principle of true health, or spirit-mind-body health through my own experience. It is a joy to share this with others who also may have the heart to integrate spiritual wisdom in their lives."*

These stories shine light on the spiritual dimension of physical and mental well-being, but the spiritual eyes with which we each view the world provide an even larger window on the primary place of spirituality in all of life. It is my sense that the cultivation of the human capacity for pure and deep connection to see through our spiritual eyes is the key to the restoration of well-being, happiness, and peace in families, organizations, communities, nations, and ultimately the entire world. Accomplishing this capacity is accomplishing true spirit-centeredness and establishing a path of true harmony by which to grow together in connected relationships. Placing spiritual practice as sacred and essential in daily life and in formal education at all levels (most especially in early childhood when spiritual insight is most natural and at the highest level) for greatest immediate influence to the largest numbers of people in society is the single most loving, far-sighted, and rewarding commitment we can make today. I pray that this capacity for deep connection, accompanied by insight, empathic communication, reflection, and realization of meaning would be rapidly developed—all the way to seeing clearly through our spiritual eyes, the window of our souls.

This path of human development explicitly includes the soul and will allow us to tap into our inherent divinity and our capacity to grasp divine truth. The resulting elevation of the mind will allow us to distinguish between the planes of human knowledge and science and divine wisdom and divine science. Seeing this distinction for ourselves will allow the striving to close the gaps in our attitudes and actions in daily life to proceed in accordance with the universal principles. The striving to link wisdom with science for posterity will follow. Thus, the paradigm of science will expand to include the whole range of subjective and objective phenomena encompassed in the universal principle of spirit-mind-body. Inner training and development common to all humanity with external training in fields and vocations in human society will be taken together with the clear understanding that spirit is first and belongs on the highest plane, with mind and body following naturally on the material plane.

My prayer is that those meant to lead the way for humanity to make the great U-turn from material-centered innermost attitudes to spirit-centered innermost attitudes will be allowed to come together now and that our Light giving and spirit-centeredness exercises may contribute to this effort. As spirit-first communities grow together in wisdom and flourish collaboratively, we will lead the way to peace by example.

Interspirituality: Cultivating Practices of Pure Connection

As you may recall from Dr. Kurt Johnson's introduction to this book, Brother Wayne Teasdale, a 20th-century Christian monk who was also ordained in the Hindu tradition and steeped in Buddhist practice, coined the term "interspirituality" to describe a shift in the spiritual development of humanity he saw on the horizon as he neared the end of his earthly life. In his 1999 book *The Mystic Heart: Discovering a Universal Spirituality in the World's Religions*, Brother Wayne (as he was affectionately known) pointed to "the realization that although there are many spiritual paths, a universal commonality underlies them all."[15] He described interspirituality as "the foundation that can prepare the way for an enlightened culture, and a continuing community among the religions that is substantial, vital, and creative."[16] This is precisely the larger vision I'm alluding to when I speak of moving away from material-first toward spiritual-first culture, and I agree with Wayne Teasdale that it will be made possible by widespread and deep commitment to spiritual practice.

There are many movements like Sukyo Mahikari for which spiritual practice is central to personal transformation and purification, along with collective commitment to altruism, unity, and, ultimately, divine union. I couldn't begin to list them all here, nor do I wish to endorse any particular movement over another. Only you, dear reader, can discern what spiritual practices you are called to. But I do believe everyone is called to some form of spiritual practice. We live in a time of unprecedented access to spiritual teachers, communities, and practices. As more people engage in authentic and meaningful practice, we will experience a cultural shift toward altruism, unity, and peace.

Wayne Teasdale called spiritual practice "the work of our transformation… the means of our inner growth and change toward human maturity."[17] While he was indeed a deeply religious Christian, his pure love of God led him to delve into both personal and academic study of spirituality in a multifaith context. In the final years of his life (Brother Wayne passed away at the age of 59 in 2004), he pointed the way forward toward a more unified society in which members of various religions share in one another's practices with acceptance, reverence, and love. He emphasized the importance of having a "disciplined habit of relating to the divine" insisting that "without a spiritual practice of some kind, spirituality is a hollow affair."[18] He set a high standard for daily spiritual practice as "the technology of inner change," emphasizing both the need for change and the necessity of practice, because "without it, such change is inconceivable." He pointed to Thomas Merton as a fellow Catholic whose daily contemplative practice equipped him to become a great teacher to millions, and Teasdale himself was mentored closely by Thomas Keating, the Trappist monk who developed the meditative method of Centering Prayer so ordinary people would have access to contemplative practices that had been preserved over centuries in monastic communities.

This contemplative dimension of Christianity can be traced back to early Christian hermits, ascetics, and monks known as the Desert Fathers and Mothers—who left mainstream society to develop deeply spiritual lives in the Egyptian desert in the early third century. During the mid-twentieth century, a group of Christian monks of the rather austere Trappist order began writing about the deep meditative practices that had been preserved over centuries in monastic communities, and then created programs by which ordinary lay people could begin to practice them as well. Thomas Merton and Thomas Keating are among the most well-known of these monks. Keating's Centering Prayer is a silent, still meditation practice by which practitioners consent to the transformative action and will of God within. Through this surrendered state, practiced twice a day for at least twenty minutes per "sit," Centering Prayer elevates the minds of ordinary practitioners to higher levels of consciousness, which can ultimately lead toward divine union.

Wayne Teasdale was not only a disciple of Thomas Keating and a practitioner of Centering Prayer, but as an interspiritual pioneer, he also engaged in many Hindu and Buddhist spiritual practices. The Interspiritual Age to which Teasdale pointed has begun to come to fruition in the two decades since his death. Thomas Keating and Wayne Teasdale's friend and colleague Dr. Kurt Johnson, who is both a former Episcopal monk and an evolutionary scientist, has written extensively on the evolution of interreligious dialogue toward interfaith action and interspiritual unity. His work is part of a global consciousness that motivates a rapidly growing number of people representing all of the world's spiritual and religious traditions, many of whom personally embrace multiple belongings. In his 2013 book *The Coming Interspiritual Age*, Kurt Johnson embraces the inherent unity found in the shared mystical understandings of all authentic spiritual paths, as well as scientific studies of consciousness and brain/mind evolution, all in the context of evolutionary views of history that recognize the impact of globalization and multiculturism. Most striking about

Johnson's work is that his deep spiritual insights are perfectly congruent with secular and scientific studies of evolutionary theory as he witnesses the ways the parallel lines of science and spirituality come together and merge in the grand reunion of mind and spirit currently underway.

Dan Siegel's mindsight work, which involves self-awareness, empathy, and integration of distinct differentiated parts in the mind and brain, sits comfortably beside Kurt Johnson's elucidations on Wayne Teasdale's descriptions of the profound self-knowledge that saints and seekers of every tradition have cultivated through spiritual practice. Siegel says mindsight is activated through the practice of reflection in attuned relationships. It develops neural circuitry in the brain and integrated nervous system throughout the body, especially in the heart and gut, allowing the sensing of mental experience and deeper truth. This neural circuitry is very different from that which is needed to see and understand physical and mechanical objects and systems in the world—learning from the outside in.[19] Inner knowing involves inside-out learning—knowing through a bottom-up sense rising up through our bodies and integrated nervous systems to our brain. It brings online our capacities for instinct, introspection, insight, inspiration, and intuition. In many ways, mindsight is to mental evolution what interspirituality is to spiritual evolution.

As a psychologist I have seen the gap between secular study of the mind and spiritual tending of the soul begin to diminish over the course of my career. Dan Siegel's work with mindsight shows that by reflecting and relating to other people in closely attuned, connected relationships, we "feel felt" and give others the experience of "feeling felt." This experience of feeling felt is a cornerstone of robust mental health and well-being and contributes to the development of humanity.[20] Similarly, our interoceptive, reflective capacities for deep inside-out learning develop through spiritual practice. We become more socially and emotionally available as we cultivate our spiritual intelligence. Our minds elevate in purity and we see psychological, spiritual, and eventually divine meaning in daily experiences. We evolve our mind's capacity to directly see connection with truth and directly feel connection with the vibration of our own innermost attitudes and true selves and those of others. Our socio-emotional intelligence begins to evolve, listening to our true selves, the true selves of others, and listening to God. This integrates the capacities of our reflective mind for felt connection and seen connection, putting it on a growing path. Our mind begins to see itself clearly, perceive and understand deep meaning in both our and others' life experiences, and thus use and integrate and continually develop synapses in the deep structures of the human brain's prefrontal cortex—referred to by Dan Siegel as the cortex humanitas.[21]

Correspondingly, our reflective capacity can deepen and become infinitely in tune with the divine as we give and receive Light. Deep and authentic spiritual practice allows us access to realizations that deepen our mind's capacity for progressive levels of illumination. The felt experience of these realizations is that their vibrational quality is very high, meaningful, and imbued with pure love. We could refer to this deep insight as "illumined mindsight." Or perhaps we should call it "divine sight", being the fruit of seeing through our spiritual eyes with the torchlight of the soul illumining the mind. Such perception and understanding attunes us step by step with progressive levels in God's will, prayer, and love. As our minds grow more pure through daily spiritual practice and living daily life in tune with the divine principles, our minds develop the capacity to see spiritual meaning in daily life experiences. Gradually, the depth of this capacity grows. We become entrusted to know progressive levels of meaning and wisdom from the spiritual to the divine. And this wisdom is transmitted instantaneously.

Through our experiences of spiritual development, our capacity for reflection, empathy, and integration can thus progress at all three levels of spirit, mind, and body, allowing us to return to connection with our own divinity. Returning to our true self is returning to our divinity, our origin, our relationship with God and to the sacred divine laws governing every aspect of existence on every plane—spiritual, mental, physical; divine, astral, material; or heaven, sky, earth. It is through this conscious spiritual reconnection that our integrated minds and bodies will also be in harmony with God's will for a peaceful spiritual civilization. So significant is the purpose of this reconnection for the human family's evolution, not only in harmony with nature, but following the example of nature. To the degree that we are always accepting and in tune with God's will, we will find peace and well-being and happiness.

The United Church of Christ has a welcome banner flying outside many of its places of worship that reads "God is still speaking." The slogan is based upon a quote attributed to comedian Gracie Allen who is said to have written her husband (George Burns) a note that he found upon her death that read as follows: "Never place a period where God has placed a comma." This message applies to the many spiritual and religious movements that have emerged in recent decades. The closed-minded notion that God communicated directly with and through chosen people like Siddhartha Gautama (the Buddha), Moses, Mary and Jesus of Nazareth, Muhammad, and through Himalayan sages and saints of many traditions—but then fell forever mute has contributed to many generations of deafness to the divine. Those who recognize that "God is still speaking" gain access not only to ancient wisdom, but modern revelations as well.

The twentieth century produced many significant teachings (some of which have roots in ancient and indigenous spirituality) which have been revealed through contemporary saints and visionaries. Sukyo Mahikari emerged in the middle of the twentieth century, when Kōtama Okada received the divine revelation that would be the basis of a new movement. He was in good company, as God revealed the importance of spiritual practice to many others in this same era. While some traditionalists eschew modern revelations as somehow less significant or less trustworthy than ancient accounts of previous revelations, I'd like to recognize a trend in the profound and pure messages that characterize many twentieth-century spiritual movements: transformation comes through daily, dedicated spiritual practice.

Again, I do not wish to endorse one movement over another, and I recognize that this time period also produced some profoundly corrupt and misguided movements by which charlatans stole many people's money and even their lives. Discernment is essential when considering the purity and authenticity of any spiritual or religious movement. But if Brother Wayne Teasdale's interspiritual vision holds true, we can expect to see some alignment between the wave of movements—with both ancient and modern roots—that are grounded and based in a solid commitment to spiritual practice.

My Prayer for Us All

So, dear reader, as we come to the end of this book, I leave you with a warm welcome to integrate spiritual practice in your daily life. The new frontier is deep within. The interspiritual movement of our time offers many true paths to reach this frontier. Some paths are ancient, some are indigenous, and some are new. If you haven't already, consider taking one up with all your heart and make it a part of your daily life. There are so many spiritual practices in my life from my spiritual path that I have come to truly love. I love reading a daily prayer to our ancestors. I love radiating Light every day to purify the environment. I love harmonizing together with family and friends at monthly thanksgiving ceremonies for God. And I love giving and receiving Light for whatever amount of time is possible each day.

Your spiritual actions will elevate the condition of your soul and the vibration of your innermost attitude to harmonize with God and universal laws. You surely have had many spiritual experiences of your own—perhaps felt connection with God, your true self, with the true selves of others, and the spiritual essence in nature and all things. Let your life progress and advance through ups and downs ameliorated and smoothened by active service to God. Let your heart of service in the world open wide to center in your true purpose, making the world a better place for everyone. Know that everything you love to do, when done selflessly, is part of that true purpose you were meant to fulfill. Let the joys that flow to you from fulfillment of true purpose overflow from your heart to heart of the world.

Daily spiritual practice, reflection through your life's ups and downs, and the trusted community of family, friends, and larger community members who are also sincerely making spiritual practice a part of their daily lives will solidify three vital planes of relationships in your life. The first relationship is with God. An unseen, great, ineffable, presence—though vast–still always within our experience in every minute part of our daily life.

The second relationship is with our true self—that luminous, eternal, divine core of energy deep within each and every one of us that anyone can see as I was blessed to see. The true self is our true common ground and our basis of being siblings in one big human family, as well as our source of equality beneath many layers of diversity. Know this truth for yourself, for it is this knowing that will open the path of living peacefully as equals in this world. Know that each of us is different and equal, each person's presence gives something to the whole that is necessary, not only for the outer progression of society, but for the inner elevation of human wisdom. Such realization will dissolve materialism and competitiveness, allowing gratitude, acceptance, and humility to grow.

The third relationship is with the true self of those with whom we are closely connected, those with whom we are distantly connected, and those who we do not know. We can connect with the essence in all things, from nature to technology. Conscious nurturing and development of all three planes of relationships will break through secular, ideational, and ideological barriers and blocks to allow experience, perception, and deep understanding to evolve.

For the mind to elevate. For the torchlight of the soul to shine through the mind's eye, allowing us to see through the window of the soul. For the first time, we will see personal and impersonal truth converge through the window of our soul and we will discern it to be the will of God. Our motivations, thoughts, and daily actions will be on the side of love, cooperation, and harmony with each other and stewardship of the earth.

For those of you who are young with life's great potential ahead of you, what could be more empowering than proactive, spiritual, evolutionary action? Already the most open-hearted of generations to walk this planet, you and your peers will grow to the full potential of your selflessness. You will care more deeply than you already do. You will see meaning in experience more clearly and you will experience the vibrations in your soul and in those with whom you interact. You will learn how to transform and elevate vibrations and thoughts to attune with the divine, ever present in every moment of daily life. Life will be richer, less lonely, less scary, less insecure. More imbued with love, more filled with hope. You will know for yourselves that the source of everything in your lives flows to you from God, through your ancestors and by divine arrangements. You will embrace opportunities to live closely with your families in daily life. Caring for and being cared for across generations, you will be whole. Your wisdom and discerning actions toward nature and all existence will ensure your well-being without impinging on anyone else's. Warmth and fulfillment will emanate through you to others. And your development as human beings in spirit, mind, and body will steer your destiny toward true health, deep harmony, and enduring prosperity. Your resulting happiness will be true.

May you make God smile. May you make the earth breathe in peace. And may we live as one human family on earth. This is my humble prayer for you, dear reader, and for the world.

Chapter 5

Spotlights

Suchandra Banerjee

As I delve into spirituality, I realize it is inherent in the human mind to seek to connect with God. Some connect through their religion, others through art and music. As you seek you find. For some the road is straight and for the others it could be long and windy. But if you seek with an earnest heart and are balanced in your approach, slowly and steadily you can reach your goal. In the words of the bard Rabindranath Tagore, when we learn to love wholeheartedly the cobwebs in our minds clear. When we cleanse our inner self and are righteous, we see that life itself is a miracle, which unfolds daily in myriad ways. Every religion teaches love and tolerance and once you seek earnestly the path unfolds in a unique way revealing the meaning, purpose, and direction to follow. As said in the Vedas, the path leads us from untruth to truth, from darkness to light, and from death to immortality. In "Growing Together in Wisdom" many have related the miracles they experienced through their strong convictions, faith, and concentration. Like locks are never manufactured without keys, similarly with patience and strong faith, the key or solution reveals. We need to turn to the omnipresent, benevolent Lord with gratitude in our hearts and sincerely seek the ultimate truth.

Kate Sheehan Roach

I first learned about giving and receiving True Light through a deeply respected friend and colleague, but even if I had not had prior knowledge of the practices and principles of Sukyo Mahikari, Leena Banerjee Brown's interspiritual approach would have drawn me right into the conversation. As a spiritual practitioner in the contemplative Christian tradition, I recognize echoes of words attributed to Jesus of Nazareth: "You are the Light of the world" and "Truly you will do even greater things than these" throughout the pages of this powerful, pure, profound, and practical book. I'm grateful to be living in this interspiritual age wherein all of the great wisdom traditions are beginning to converge in an evolutionary leap toward world unity and peace—the Great U-turn we've been praying for and working toward. This final chapter reads like a benediction to me, as the author graciously shines God's Light as a blessing upon us all.

Kusumita P. Pederson

In True Light Leena Banerjee Brown skillfully weaves her own personal narrative and stories of her family and friends together with a clear and searching explanation of the teachings of Sukyo Mahikari. She describes how the giving and receiving of Light heals and enlightens spirit, mind and body and over time shifts our priority from the material to the spiritual. This process is an integral spirituality as it unites spirit, mind and body and brings together inner wisdom with external knowledge. The author draws on her expertise as a psychologist to give insight into how this process works. Fulfilment comes in living according to universal principles and in altruistic love, empathy, humility, and gratitude. Equally important, she shows that harmony with the Earth and the betterment of society are intrinsic to this spiritual path. In closing she opens the perspective of the Sukyo Mahikari way of Light to the global movement of Interspirituality and connection with contemplative practices and ethics of other traditions. True Light is a vivid and compelling account of spiritual seeking and finding – offered in a spirit of hope and care for a world in desperate need of transformation.

Afterword

Light, in the world's spiritual traditions, represents divine presence, transcendence, and our ability to see beyond the seen. In some traditions, Light is what gives us the ability to see into our own true nature and discover our deepest identity as reflections of the one all-encompassing Light itself. This divine Light permeates the entire universe as the spiritual energy or vibration of the Creator's unconditional love for the entire creation. Light is our lasting identity, but the things of the world can cause us to forget this is who we are. Leena Banerjee Brown and her collaborators show here that practicing the art of *True Light* not only reminds us who we are, but can also transform our lives.

The remarkable stories shared by ordinary people who have embarked upon the spiritual journey express what many of us are also witnessing and living in this challenging time. So much needs to be attended to, treated, and recovered from as we become who we are intended to be—filled with and acting upon our own wisdom, love, and altruism—allowing us to live with a deep and authentic sense of purpose.

These experiences recall the universal motifs and archetypes that make up Joseph Campbell's outline of the pattern of transformation drawn from the world's mythology, the archetypes first seen in the stories of the gods and goddesses of ancient times that still show up in our own lives today. We notice these universal archetypes especially as we respond to opportunities for change that are given to us. These moments of chaos, loss, or separation are necessary to lead us through other moments of assistance, further challenges, and greater awakenings. These universal experiences propel us, through all adversity, toward renewal and rebirth, reminding us that we are always whole beings, connected, through our spiritual nature, to the Creator. Experiences of profound connection with the infinite are shared throughout the pages of *True Light*, repeatedly showing us how we are all linked to each other through such deeply human potentials.

Throughout this practical and prayerful book is also evidence of built-in connections between the spiritual practices and universal principles of Sukyo Mahikari and other modern holistic movements—as well as with the world's great wisdom traditions, confirming what Wayne Teasdale foresaw as a broadening recognition of a universal spirituality emerging from within and across all traditions. And even in the mid-20th century, the personal spiritual evolution of its founder, Kōtama Okada, leading to a calling to establish a spiritual movement, can be seen to mirror the motifs and archetypes of direct personal experience of the infinite found in the lives of the great prophets and spiritual leaders across time.

It is always these similarities, universals, and deeply held human ideals transcending artificial barriers that attract those of different traditions, create lasting bonds, and offer a holistic perspective of human progress pointing to wholeness and unity that gives us all hope for the future.

The spiritual life is our common journey that inevitably leads to a better place. Through daily dedicated spiritual practice, such as the art of True Light, this journey takes us to deeper levels of self-awareness, empathy, integration, relationship, and connectedness, ultimately reminding us of our own divinity. This aligns us with the universal laws and principles that order all elements of the entire creation.

A solid commitment to spiritual practice offers us our own path to a direct experience of "interspirituality," the holistic perspective that resides at the mystic heart of the world's sacred traditions. This awareness of the interconnectedness of all things enables both our own and humanity's collective transformation and evolution to progress toward the "peaceful spiritual civilization" envisioned here and by so many across many centuries, a beautiful reminder of who we are and what we are made for.

Dr. Robert Atkinson, 2021

Acknowledgements

My deepest gratitude to the numerous presences, seen and unseen, in the family, in the editorial-publishing team, among friends, and in the community, who have embraced and facilitated the publication of this book. Thank you. I am ever grateful for the sincerity and selfless actions of all spiritual practitioners, including Sukyo Mahikari staff and practitioners. What more can any of us do than to strive as human beings with our families to truly reclaim our souls and grow together spiritually in harmony with the earth? Thank you for your daily efforts. Thank you to those who have let me tell your stories along with mine. Thank you to those who have written your comments in this book. Your words bring joy. My hope is that we will together inspire and move the hearts and souls of readers to transform daily life on the planet to spirit-centeredness and true harmony.

Contributors

Dr. Robert Atkinson, an award-winning author, speaker, and developmental psychologist, is an internationally recognized authority on life story interviewing, a pioneer in personal mythmaking, and professor emeritus at the University of Southern Maine who has been engaged in global peace work for many years.

Dr. Liza Auciello, founder of My Best Self Coach and Elevate CE, is a licensed psychologist who helps people match their energy and emotions with their goals so they can fulfill their true purpose.

Suchandra Banerjee, whose family is originally from Bengal, lives in Noida near New Delhi, India where she invests herself in helping her neighbors, especially the younger generations, at the same time as being a proud matriarch and mother of the author.

Xiye Bastida is Mexican-Chilean, a member of the Mexican Otomi-Toltec nation, a major organizer of Fridays for Future in New York City, a leading voice for indigenous and immigrant visibility in climate activism, co-founder of Re-Earth Initiative, and a student at the University of Pennsylvania.

Dr. Roger Beck is a member of the Edmonton Sukyo Mahikari Center in Canada, a yoko farmer, and professor emeritus of economics at the University of Alberta School of Business who has generously contributed many of his life stories to this book.

Deepa Bhushan, whose family is originally from the Punjab, lives in the Kandbari region of the Himalaya in India where she has founded a children's school called Udaan. She is a lawyer, a proud mother of three young men, and a long-time friend of the author.

Gail Breakey, MPH is a member of the Sukyo Mahikari Honolulu Center in USA, founder of the child abuse prevention program Healthy Start, and a devoted advocate for early intervention who loves the aloha spirit of Hawaii.

Mira Ambika Banerjee Brown is a Sukyo Mahikari Pasadena Center member in USA and the author's daughter. She is an active catalyst for the soul-building work of supporting fourth graders in high-risk Los Angeles schools become confident people and strong readers. This work gives her real joy as does her inspired cooking for family and friends and throwing on her potter's wheel.

Girish Chandorkar, whose family is Maharashtrian, is a member of the Sukyo Mahikari Pune Center in Maharashtra, India. He retired as Principal Chief Commissioner of Income Tax and loves trekking regularly in the Himalaya.

Dekila Chungyalpa is a global voice for climate resilience and environmental justice who actively collaborates with faith and indigenous leaders and directs the Loka Initiative at the University of Wisconsin-Madison.

Dr. John Cobb is a noted theologian, philosopher and environmentalist, Professor Emeritus of Claremont Graduate University elected to the American

Academy of Arts and Sciences, and proud patriarch of four generations of his family.

Dr. Lanette Darby is a member of the Sukyo Mahikari Honolulu Center in USA, a retired educational psychologist, and a member of Circles. She loves her native home, the beautiful Hawaiian Islands, its majestic mountains, and crystal blue sea.

Dr. Karen Eastman, PhD is a psychologist committed to meditation and mind-body interventions with a private practice in Los Angeles. She has taught at the Chinese University of Hong Kong, UCLA, and UC Irvine, and is a member of Circles.

Dr. Sara Edrington is a licensed psychologist and **Sean Edrington** is a financial advisor. They both enjoy adventures and good laughs with their daughter, son, large extended family, and close friends.

Dr. Shamini Jain is a psychologist, researcher, devoted member of her intergenerational family, and founder of Consciousness Healing Initiative (CHI), a collaborative accelerator to advance the science and practice of healing, that is wholeness.

Dr. Kurt Johnson has engaged deeply in a dual career involving science and spirituality for over forty years, through which he has been instrumental in connecting people in cultivating an evolutionary worldview, a global interspiritual community, and a more collaborative and reciprocal partnership ethic.

Deb Mukharji, IFS, retired as Indian Ambassador to Nepal and lives in New Delhi. He has been expressing his great love for the Himalaya by walking there with his camera for more than six decades. His photographs, published in numerous journals and acclaimed at exhibitions, have appeared in the two books he has authored on Nepal as well as two he has written about the Kailas-Manas region.

Amaranta Nehru is a member of the Sukyo Mahikari New Delhi Center in India and lives with her husband in the city. Her family, originally from Kashmir, has a Goshintai (holy scroll) of Creator God enshrined in their home in Pune. She is a visual artist who uses art as a developmental tool to mentor design students as she strives to integrate the spiritual life and the artistic life.

Kate Sheehan Roach, MA is an editor, writer, and historian who is committed to cultivating the contemplative dimension of life for the betterment of all creation. She loves to walk among the tall trees near her home with her husband, daughter, son, and their big yellow dog, Woods. It has been her great honor to serve as developmental editor of this book.

Kusumita P. Pedersen is Professor Emerita of Religious Studies, St. Francis College. She is co-author of Global Ethics in Practice: Historical Backgrounds, Current Issues and Future Prospects and co-author of Faith for Earth: A Call to Action. Kusumita has also compiled and edited librettos for two works by Philip Glass: Symphony No. 5: Bardo, Requiem and Nirmānakāya (1999) and The Passion of Ramakrishna (2006). She has been active in the interfaith movement for over thirty years and now focuses much of her work on climate change.

Pooja Verma applies the tools offered by Sadhguru and the Isha Foundation to strengthen her spiritual practice and nourish her well-being, and on warm, breezy days she enjoys sitting in the sun with her fluffy dog Waffles and the three generations of wonderful women in her family.

About the Author

Leena Banerjee Brown, PhD, was born and raised in India. She is Bengali and is currently a member of the Sukyo Mahikari Pasadena Center in the United States. A licensed psychologist, she retired from her career as professor of clinical psychology at Alliant International University. Throughout her career she served children and families in underserved communities in India and the United States, including in New Delhi, Honolulu, and Los Angeles. She trained graduate students to become clinicians, guided their doctoral research, and clinically supervised younger colleagues preparing for professional licensure. These collaborations focused on self-awareness development, family therapy, multicultural psychology, early intervention, and community mental health—fields in which she contributed to the scholarly literature as well.[22] She raised and nurtured her children and family in the United States, making regular trips with them to be with family in India.

Becoming a Sukyo Mahikari practitioner has given the author the opportunity to develop self-awareness that transcends the realm of the mind to touch the pristine, powerful depths of the soul. She retired from her career in order to concentrate on cultivating this depth through divine service and co-founded the Circles group to invite leaders to share in giving and receiving Light and reflecting together. She also sowed the intention in her heart to write about spiritual experiences and divine wisdom; this book is the first materialization of this intent. The work of fostering spiritual growth is what she now loves to do most, and to see and feel God's Light reflected in family life and in closely connected relationships gives her great joy. There is no work more urgent to her than the elevation of human goodness, virtue, and spiritual condition through disciplined spiritual practice in daily life. She sees that spiritual elevation will allow human actions to be in tune with divine will, which will ensure durable resilience in people, families, environmental work, social justice, evolution of self-awareness and selflessness, true happiness, and peace. These are the hopes she holds in her heart as she gives and receives Light.

Endnotes

1. See, for instance, at Contemplative Life: https://community. contemplativelife.org/articles/interspiritual-visions

2. Extract from "The Holy Words" English edition, 2002, p. 4.

3. The ritual tests are called tenjo. They involve a special technique of automatic writing in which a writing brush is suspended from a pole held at either end by a Shinto priest.

4. The mission of sumei godo.

5. The mission of yosuka judo.

6. See, for instance http://www.thecominginterspiritualage.com/ interspiritual-pioneers and http://multiplex.isdna.org/classica. htm#photo%20archive at one of the original Wayne Teasdale websites.

7. Mary Helen Immordino-Yang, Emotions, Learning and the Brain: Exploring the Educational Implications of Affective Neuroscience (New York: W.W. Norton, 2016).

8. Jared Diamond, Collapse: How Societies Chose to Fail or Succeed (New York: Viking Press, 2005).

9. See www.prosocial.world and community.prosocial.world/prosocial-spirituality for training programs supporting this evolutionary convergence of science and spirituality.

10. Stephen J. Genuis, "The Chemical Erosion of Human Health: Adverse Environmental Exposure and In-utero Pollution—Determinants of Congenital Disorders and Chronic Disease," J. Perinat. Med. 34 (2006).

11. K. Kunii, "Gratitude for Oshienushisama's visits to the earthquake disaster areas, reforming our souls, and miraculous protection against nuclear radiation," Sukyo Mahikari International Journal, June, No. 119, (2012) 29-34.

12. Daniel Cressey, "Widely Used Herbicide Linked to Cancer," Nature, March 24 (2015).

13. Thirty years later, I'm happy to say that Project Tiger was successful.

14. CD Lorish and R.Maisiak., "The Face Scale," Arthritis Rheum 29 (1996), 906-909.

15. Wayne Teasdale, The Mystic Heart: Discovering a Universal Spirituality in the World's Religions (Novato, California: New World Library, 1999), p. 25.

16. Ibid, p. 26.

17. Ibid, p. 128.

18. Ibid, p.128.

19. Daniel Siegel, Pocket Guide to Interpersonal Neurobiology (New York: W.W. Norton & Co., Inc. 2012), p. 22.

20. Daniel Siegel, The Developing Mind: How Relationships and Brain Interact to Shape Who We Are, second edition (New York: The Guilford Press, 2012).

21. Daniel Siegel, Mindsight: The New Science of Personal Transformation (New York: Bantam Books, 2010).
    Ibid.

22. Leena Banerjee and Michelle Willingham, "Self Awareness Development," Journal of Research and Applications in Clinical Psychology, 1(2), (1998),1-

    Leena Banerjee, "Self Development Practices for Professionals, Gems from the Family Therapy Field," Psychological Foundations, The Journal, Vol 11, (2), December, (2000), 48-54.

    Leena Banerjee and Janet Sawyers, "The Double-Bind: An Empirical Study of Responses to Inconsistent Communications," Journal of Marital and Family Therapy, 12(4), (1986), 395-402.

    Leena Banerjee and Janet Sawyers, "Interpreting Subtle Inconsistency and Consistency: A Developmental-Clinical Perspective", Journal of Genetic Psychology, 151 (4), (1990), 515-521.

    Leena Banerjee, "Dress as a Manifest Aspect of Identity: An Indian American Narrative," J. Chin (Ed.), The Psychology of Prejudice and Discrimination, Vol 4. (Westport CT: Praeger Press, 2004).

Leena Banerjee Brown, Circles in the Nursery: Practicing Multicultural Family Therapy, (Washington, DC: Zero to Three Press, 2007).

Leena Banerjee, "Through a Child's Eyes: What's in a Name and Other Thoughts on Social Categorizations in America," The Community Psychologist, 33 (2), (2000), 16-18.